ROB KORNBLUM

NEVER TOO LATE TO STARTUP

HOW MID-LIFE ENTREPRENEURS
CREATE WEALTH, FREEDOM & PURPOSE

NEVER TOO LATE TO STARTUP
How Mid-Life Entrepreneurs Create
Wealth, Freedom & Purpose

ISBN   978-1-61961-420-8 *Paperback*
          978-1-61961-421-5 *Ebook*

LIONCREST
PUBLISHING

NEVER TOO LATE TO STARTUP

CONTENTS

DOWNLOAD THE
BONUSES FREE!

Thank you for buying the book.

I have assembled a significant amount of free resources to help you on your entrepreneurial journey. Please visit http://www. startlaunchgrow.com/nevertoolate-bonuses to get access to all the bonus resources below.

- One Page Business Plan template—get started with the ideal short form plan, ideal for new companies; complete it in hours
- Marketing template—how to position any company, product, or blog
- Worksheet for building your ideal culture and values
- Resources—links to many of the tools and resources that mid-life entrepreneurs use to launch their companies and simplify their lives
- Pitch Deck template—built by a former venture capitalist
- Blueprint for creating a basic financial plan
- Ninety day action plan to get started on your business
- And more...

INTRODUCTION

THIS BOOK IS FOR YOU

*"The greatest danger for most of us is
not that our aim is too high and we miss
it, but that it is too low and we reach it."*

MICHELANGELO

Joe Williams was frustrated. Last year, he sat down at his computer to go over his finances. His 401(k) account was up; that was the good news. The bad news was that it still hadn't recovered from its decline in 2008 and 2009. In 2010, Joe lost his job as a project manager for a large oil company. It took him five months to find a new job, during which time his savings took a beating.

Joe's new job pays well, though not quite as well as his old job. His wife works part time, but her hours were just cut back, which puts a real dent in their income. On top of that, Joe's health insurance premiums are going to increase by more than 10 percent next year.

He can pay his bills, but his retirement and college savings plans are way behind. He shakes his head thinking about college for his two daughters. They're smart and could probably be accepted to elite private universities, but how would he pay for it?

Joe has been considering an idea for a new business startup. As a professional project manager, he has always struggled to find easy-to-use management tools. He's tried them all, and he has solid ideas for better solutions. He's been mulling it over for almost six years. He's an avid watcher of *Shark Tank*, the reality TV series in which aspiring entrepreneurs pitch a panel of potential investors called "sharks." He also subscribes to *Inc.* magazine.

Joe is seriously considering going into business for himself, but he's still not sure. Could he really pull it off, starting a company at age forty three? Aren't startups for young kids right out of college?

STARTING UP IN MID-LIFE

I wrote this book for people who've been working for awhile and want to start their own businesses, people I call "mid-life" entrepreneurs. If you're in your late thirties, forties, or perhaps into your fifties, and you've been thinking about starting your own company, *Never Too Late to Startup* is for you.

This book came about to fill a need.

I'd been running my own startup located in an incubator when I noticed that most of my peer CEOs were in their twenties, significantly younger than I. I was struck by how differently they did everything, from the hours they worked to how they approached team-building, raising money, and working with customers. I started blogging about it and discovered a whole world of mid-life entrepreneurs out there who needed to know more about how to start a business later in life.

What they needed and wanted was a real-world field guide geared specifically for mid-life entrepreneurs.

In these pages you'll meet successful mid-life CEOs and company founders who've done exactly what you're about to do. Their startup stories apply at every level of career, particularly mid-career and even later as today's retirees increasingly venture out on their own.

Mid-life entrepreneurs already have a few decades of work and life experience. Like you, they have significant professional skills, typically a large and valuable network, and the motivation to build something for themselves and their families.

Your own hard-earned professional experience and skills are huge benefits when applied to building a new business. Skills such as hiring, organization, planning, communication, selling, and negotiating all improve with time and age. They are invaluable advantages as you start your first company in mid-life or mid-career.

WHERE ARE YOU RIGHT NOW?

Becoming a mid-life entrepreneur poses some unique and significant challenges. Mid-life founders don't just need the right business idea; they need to find the time in an already full life to assess, execute, and manage all the details of their new company.

Contrary to popular media clichés, no one comes out of the womb a born entrepreneur. Sure, some people are more comfortable with risk than others. Some kids are more inclined to ski the double black diamonds. But much in life is learned and earned along the way.

So, where are you right now?

You're in your forties (or something like that) and you feel you're finally ready to start a company. You had good reasons to not do it sooner. You were building a career, learning your trade, making money, climbing the corporate ladder, or just living your life.

It doesn't matter why you didn't start a company in your twenties. What matters is that you're ready now. You have the ideas, the maturity, the skills, the motivation, and maybe some savings. You've built up a tolerance for risk, and you're ready to learn new things.

The entrepreneurs you'll meet in *Never Too Late to Startup* could pretty much be you. They weren't born yesterday and they brought established skills and experience to the table. They weren't huge risk takers. In my interviews with them, they expressed measured and thoughtful approaches to launching new products, hiring people, and spending money.

TRANSFORM YOUR LIFE, CHANGE THE WORLD

You are about to embark on a journey in which you take control of your work. You'll control what you work on, who you work with, what hours you work, where you work, and what impact you're going to have on the world.

It might seem far-fetched—the idea that you can impact the world with your new business. But it's really not.

Maybe you're looking to build a technology company that will change the way people communicate or work, or a game that millions of people will use. Or maybe you're going into business as a consultant or blogger so you can spread your knowledge and skills.

As your business succeeds and grows, you'll be impacting more people. The first time you hire a new employee, you'll feel it in your gut—that sense of responsibility for someone else's financial well-being. You'll want your business to succeed and grow that much more. And trust me, it'll feel entirely different than hiring staff in a corporate job on someone else's dime and company name.

As you follow the stories of entrepreneurs on these pages and learn the ins and outs of starting your own business, you'll see why I believe that entrepreneurs are made, not born. There is no entrepreneur gene, only tried and true ways to get there.

All you need is a guide, which is why I wrote *Never Too Late to Startup.*

I believe that people get better at starting companies, coming up with ideas, launching products, and hiring people the more they do it. Starting a business involves distinct skills and attitudes, just like everything else in life. You just have to exercise the right muscles to operate at your best.

You're about to transform your life, and maybe the world. On these pages you'll be finding out that not only is it *Never Too Late to Startup*, but the best time is now.

WHY YOU NEED TO BE AN ENTREPRENEUR

———

"Do not lose hold of your dreams or aspirations. For if you do, you may still exist but you have ceased to live."

HENRY DAVID THOREAU

The traditional path is not getting you to where you want to be. Deep down inside you know it. We have all been conditioned by teachers, parents, and friends who told us to study, get a good job, work hard, pay our dues, and rise to the upper middle class or better.

Maybe you aren't satisfied with the traditional path. Corporate life, with its overall lack of control, all its rules and procedures, just isn't for you. Maybe you're tired of all those coworkers who don't seem to care and still get ahead. You feel like yelling,

"Why did that guy get a bonus *and* a promotion?"

You've tried the traditional way. You invested in a house and the stock market only to see your wealth rise and fall with the economic times. Perhaps you've improved your standing somewhat, but it's often a case of one step forward, two steps back. It certainly was for me!

Maybe you got laid off in the Great Recession of late 2007 to mid-year 2009, like I did. Or maybe it was the bursting of the tech bubble in 2001. You might have suffered through losing your house or seeing friends or relatives lose theirs. Or maybe your company outsourced your job and you had to train the replacement.

Or maybe your job just bores you. You crave meaning and purpose in your work and the chance to build something.

A NEW WORLD OF WORK

If you're like most Americans, you're working harder and taking fewer vacations. Your income is stagnant or declining, you have relatively few retirement assets, and you most definitely *do not* feel like you're getting ahead.

You have absolutely no idea how you'll pay for college for your kids. You want to give your kids the same advantages you had, right? But $60,000 a year for college? Seriously?

We're facing perhaps the most difficult financial time in modern history. The Great Depression of the 1930s was devastating but temporary. It was followed by decades of growth and prosperity after World War II and the birth of the middle class.

But the challenges that face us today appear to be permanent and systemic. Globalization isn't going away. The growth in new technologies is increasing, not decreasing.

The institutions and systems we've depended on have all shifted under our feet. Job creation has stagnated along with wages. Wealth creation through the stock market has become harder and harder to achieve. Buy-and-hold doesn't really work when you have deep bear markets that produce significant losses.

These trends are creating seismic shifts in the economy and marketplace. Yet today's challenges are also creating massive opportunity for entrepreneurs. Let's take a look at these challenges and trends so we can find the alternate routes to success.

WHERE DID THE MONEY GO?

If you look at the data, you'll begin to understand that the old way was a lie for most people.

Over the last twenty five years, wages for 95 percent of Americans have stagnated. The United States economy has generally grown, even with the significant recession of 2007 to 2009, but wages have not kept pace. Real median household income has declined since 2000. A rising economy should help create jobs and create income and wealth. So what happened?

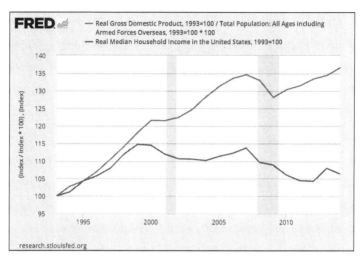

US. Bureau of Economic Analysis, Real Gross Domestic Product [GDPC1], retrieved from FRED, Federal Reserve Bank of St. Louis https://research.stlouisfed.org/fred2/series/GDPC1

What happened is household income declined while Gross Domestic Product, the output of the United States economy, went up. This wasn't always the case.

From 1948 to 2000, jobs grew faster than the United States population. This made finding a high-quality job easier, and wages went up. But during the last fifteen years we've seen a fundamental shift in our pattern of job growth. From 2000 to today, the number of jobs created has simply not kept pace with our growth in population.

Part of the reason for wage stagnation is that more and more people are *under*employed.

The Great Recession produced huge decreases in employment,

some 8.8 million jobs lost. And although employment has largely returned to pre-recession levels, the new jobs are largely unskilled and don't pay the same level of wages as before.

You see college graduates working at Starbucks or Gap. These might be good jobs for some workers, but not for people with special skills or college degrees.

Underemployment is also a factor when the only jobs available are part time instead of full time. We all know people—sometimes ourselves!—who had good, high-paying jobs with titles and benefits before the Great Recession and now have to settle for much less.

The experts have highlighted the problem of underemployment as well. According to a 2014 *Forbes Magazine* article, the unemployed and underemployed rate remained stubbornly in the 14 percent range as late as 2013. Professor Robert Pollin commented, "There is employment...[but] it's starkly concentrated at the top."[1]

The pressures on families are real. The challenges and trends in underemployment today go beyond political party. We all have to deal with these changes no matter our political persuasion.

THE CHALLENGE OF SAVING FOR COLLEGE

As a parent, you probably feel as I do: you want your kids to have the advantage of a college degree. Saving for college is a huge financial pressure that pushes our need to earn more. But no matter how much we try to save, tuition keeps rising faster both for public and private schools.

You certainly want to help put your kids through school—a college degree is mandatory for most good jobs. College has gone from "nice to have" to "must have" in the competition for jobs.

The Hamilton Project has documented dramatically rising tuition at all institutions. Four year private colleges have increased more than twelve times since 1980, and they are projected to keep rising faster than wages or inflation.[2]

Kids and parents are taking on more debt to cover these incredible costs. Student loan debt is the fastest rising form of debt in the United States. Loan debt rose 84 percent from 2008 to 2014 and is the only type of personal debt to increase during that time. There are now more than $1.2 trillion in outstanding student loans.[3]

Why are students and parents taking on these staggering loans? According to a study of Labor Department statistics conducted by the Economic Policy Institute,[4] college graduates with four-year degrees make 98 percent more an hour than people without a degree. Virtually every non-hourly job requires a bachelor's degree as part of the screening process.

If you're like me, you probably started thinking about saving early on in your child's life, only to watch your ability to pay for college shrink as tuition skyrocketed.

WILL I EVER BE ABLE TO RETIRE?

Our ability to save for retirement is becoming ever more elusive.

In 1979, 62 percent of employees with employer-based retirement plans had "defined-benefit" plans, or pensions. Employers contributed to a pension fund based on an employee's earnings each year. The pension paid employees a fixed amount when they retired. But by 2011, the percentage of employees who still had pension plans had shrunk to only 7 percent.

What happened to pensions?

Companies, assisted by federal law, shifted retirement savings out of pensions and into 401(k) plans to save themselves money. These new, so-called "defined contribution" plans require employees to save a percentage out of their own paychecks. The company can contribute also but doesn't have to.

The bottom line is that employers used to put aside money for an employee's retirement. Your pension was based on your final salary with the company. Now the burden of saving for retirement has shifted almost entirely to the employee.

For most people, day-to-day expenses and debt get in the way of making significant progress toward retirement savings. A vast majority of workers have less than $25,000 in 401(k) savings.

This simply isn't going to get the average person very far in retirement. Most people will need to find other ways to generate income, wealth, and savings.

THE FREELANCE ECONOMY

More and more people around the world are freelancing, or engaging in temporary, project-based work. Freelancers are independent contractors or "consultants" paid by the day, the hour, or the job. They aren't employees on payrolls. For some, it supplements their other employment, but for many, it is their only employment.

More than 54 million Americans have done freelance work in the last year, a full one-third of the workforce. Much of that work is done remotely, or "virtually," using the Internet, such as designing, writing and editing, coding, and marketing. But some services are delivered locally, in person, including house cleaning, shopping, and dog walking.

I had two long stints of consulting or freelancing. In the first case, it was a total necessity. I needed the money and permanent jobs were hard to come by. The second time was after I'd left my startup and stumbled into a freelance opportunity. It was a great way to recharge my brain, recover my confidence and sanity, and work on this book.

Why has freelancing exploded? First, it is available as a way to make more money on the side. As we explored earlier, many of us are underemployed and need additional income.

But larger technological, structural, and cultural trends are also at work. Globalization and generational shifts in the world economy are at play, including the mobility of the Internet. Jobs and work are being reshaped by these changes.

Mary Meeker, the super-smart Internet analyst and venture capital partner at Kleiner Perkins, has explored these shifts. In her 2015 report on Internet Trends, Meeker highlights the fact that "good" jobs in the production sector have declined as a percentage of total jobs from 44 percent in 1943 to 14 percent in 2014.[5]

Service jobs, in contrast, have risen from 56 percent to 86 percent in the same period. Most jobs today are predicated on paying people for a service rather than producing an item. And services are much more mobile and easily replicated on a smaller scale in a freelance setting.

Also, over the last thirty years, highly skilled jobs have grown much faster than all others. As defined by the United States Department of Labor, these "non-routine, cognitive jobs," which require creativity and problem solving, have doubled since 1983. But that leaves a lot of people out.

People and culture have changed along with the labor market. One hundred years ago, less than half of the United States population lived in urban areas. Today, more than 80 percent of Americans live in or near cities.

The marriage rate among young people has also changed; in fact, it has plunged. Only 26 percent of eighteen-to-thirty-three-year-olds in the United States are married, compared to more than 60 percent in 1960.

With a much younger, more mobile, and urban work force, the nature of work and of rewards has shifted. Millennials demand and expect more flexible hours and are increasingly bringing technology into the workforce.

Combine the labor and demographic trends with the massive increase in Internet and smartphone usage, and you have a connected, on-demand workforce. Companies like UpWork (formerly oDesk,) Uber, Airbnb, Fiverr, and others are enabling people to work on the side and earn some extra money—or their only money.

THE ENTREPRENEUR SOLUTION

With all of these economic challenges facing you, is there a clear path to something better?

Never Too Late to Startup offers a way. Becoming an entrepreneur offers you the chance to take control of your financial and professional life. This might mean quitting your job to start a company, but it might also mean starting a little business on the side.

Becoming an entrepreneur does not have to be risky and it does not have to mean quitting your job and having no means of support. We all have bills to pay.

In *Never Too Late to Startup* you'll learn:

- How to generate ideas for a new company.
- How to test those ideas.
- How to manage the legal pitfalls.
- How to set up a company properly.
- How to fund your new business.
- How to grow it.

And you'll learn to do it all in the context of the daily demands of a mid-life entrepreneur.

MYTH BUSTING

You might not yet believe that entrepreneurship is right for you. Like our family man Joe with his own project management solutions, perhaps you're unsure about starting a company. An inner voice keeps whispering about risk, planting self-doubt, telling you you're not ready.

You have some friends and family as well who are reinforcing that inner voice of doubt.

If you've been thinking about starting a company, you probably have a set of perceptions about entrepreneurship formed by media and popular culture.

Let's take a look at a few of these myths and the realities.

Myth 1: *Entrepreneurs are young.*

After all, Bill Gates, Michael Dell, and Mark Zuckerberg all dropped out of college and started their companies in their twenties. Right?

The Reality: It turns out that the highest rate of entrepreneurship can be found among fifty-five-to-sixty-four-year-olds. The "risk takers" in the twenty-to-thirty-four-year-old bracket actually have the lowest rate.[6] This is according to research conducted by The Ewing Marion Kauffman Foundation as part of its mission to support entrepreneurship in America.

This isn't just a short-term phenomenon either. For every year from 1996 to 2007, entrepreneurship was higher in the fifty-five-to-sixty-four group than in the twenty-to-thirty-four group.

But wait, what about technology startups? Isn't the high-tech economy a bastion of the young?

As it turns out, a different Kauffman Foundation study, this one authored by entrepreneur-turned-professor Vivek Wadhwa, found that the median age of successful founders of technology companies was thirty nine. There were twice as many technology founders over fifty than under twenty five.

We'll hear more from Wadhwa later. He has some strongly held opinions about mid-life founders and the benefits of experience in starting new companies.

Myth 2: *Entrepreneurs don't have families because founders work 24/7.*

The Reality: As you will see in this guide, many entrepreneurs do have families. They work hard, make it home for dinner, coach soccer, and put their kids to bed. I'm not going to tell you it's easy, or a simple nine-to-five. It isn't. But managing a family and a fledgling business is doable. It requires a balancing act of work and home, discipline and communication, and a very good support system.

Myth 3: *Starting a company is risky. Entrepreneurs are risk seekers.*

The Reality: Statistics do show that many startups fail, but there are ways to significantly reduce the risks. By choosing cofounders carefully, testing incrementally, and planning cautiously, you can overcome the odds. Most of the founders I spoke with are not risk seekers. They are smart, experienced business people who manage risk by building great teams and trying to avoid running down high-risk rat holes.

With billions of consumers available through the Internet, untold educational support, and free/cheap and accessible tools and technologies, today's environment is the best time in history to start a new business. I will cover exactly why this is so more deeply in Chapter 5.

Myth 4: *Starting a company means quitting my job.*

The Reality: The cost of starting a new company has dropped exponentially to the point that many founders start businesses on the side and test their ideas on nights and weekends. When it looks promising, they can quit their day job and seek to raise some capital. Or they might bootstrap it as their company's only employee by using inexpensive tools and contract employees.

Remember: Paying your bills doesn't have to mean sitting on your dreams and bobbing on a sea of uncertainty that is a job in corporate America today.

Myth 5: *I'm just not an entrepreneur.*

The Reality: This one is perhaps less of a myth and more of an excuse. There's more than one way to become an entrepreneur and run your own business. In *Never Too Late to Startup*, I'll outline a process that involves generating business ideas, building a framework to test your ideas, learning from that testing, building a great team, generating revenue, and eventually quitting your day job.

EXPERIENCE COUNTS

You might not know it yet, but you have everything you need to create a business and begin generating extra income and wealth for yourself and your family. You have the professional experience of managing people and projects, the personal experience to know how to persevere, the motivation, and the network to help you find customers, contractors, advice, and help.

You are better equipped to start a successful new business than the college students and twenty-something entrepreneurs. Sure, the media loves to play up the darlings who drop out of college and create a giant company, but those are astoundingly rare.

Lew Cirne has founded multiple companies. He started his

most recent company, New Relic, in his late thirties, and it has been massively successful. I think Cirne said it best about being a mid-life founder:

> I take it as a total myth that startups are for the very young, and if you're over thirty starting a company you're over the hill. Yeah, it's totally wrong. The press loves the Mark Zuckerberg story, but that's because there's like three of those people in the last ten years that have done it.

Studies have borne out the fact that professional experience increases the chances of entrepreneurial success. A study commissioned in 2009 by the Kauffman Foundation showed successful entrepreneurs were forty years old on average when they founded their companies.

Almost every element that goes into creating a successful company gets better with age and experience. When I spoke with Vivek Wadhwa, the Stanford University professor who co-authored the Kauffman Foundation study, he told me that venture capitalists looking for young entrepreneurs have it entirely wrong:

> [Overall experience] makes a big difference because [success is so based on] experience. How do you know about markets? How do you know where to look? How do you know how to manage people? How do you know how to manage finances? All of these things require experience. You aren't born with management skills and finance skills and knowledge of markets. All of this comes with experience and experience comes with age.

YOUR MOMENT OF TRUTH

Maybe you think you'll just buckle down, work harder, save more, and everything will settle out. It might, but not likely. The sand is shifting under your feet.

It's not your fault. Institutions are changing the rules even faster than you can adapt, if you keep playing their game. They've moved the goal posts on you. It's like you were in a road race, a comfortable 10K, and halfway through they changed the course. Now it's all uphill and the prize is a lot smaller.

But you don't need to play their game.

Many of the same factors that have caused these economic shifts—the explosion of technology and the Internet, globalization, tech-enabled competition—are creating the best time in the history of the world to take control of your income through entrepreneurship.

The career path of traditional companies is broken. The safety net is gone. After the economic collapse of 2008 and 2009, and the bursting of the tech bubble in 2001, we can all see that corporate America isn't a "safe" route anymore.

What happens if you turn fifty and get laid off? Or worse, what if it happens at sixty?

It is time to take control of your life and the time is now.

It's time to think like an entrepreneur.

There has never been an easier time to reach customers, a less expensive time to set up the systems and processes for running a company, a better time to learn by doing. It is all right there for you to turn your dream into reality.

I'm not suggesting that you just quit your job and start a company. The right path might be to start laying the groundwork for a side business, one you can grow and use to generate extra income. Over time your side business will grow into your main business and generate true wealth.

Laying the groundwork means doing the work. Generating ideas and doing something with them. It means coming up with a plan. It means networking to find people who can help you start up. It means testing your idea. It means writing a short business plan.

One thing it most certainly does *not* mean is staying in the same old grind.

We all have trepidation. We all have uncertainties and fears. We all have preconceptions and old habits that hold us back. We all have practical considerations—constraints of money, time, and family.

So before we jump in, let's clear the air. Let's have a look at your motivations for starting a company as well as some of the fears that might be holding you back.

WHY DO YOU WANT TO START A COMPANY?

"Ambition is the path to success.
Persistence is the vehicle you arrive in."

BILL BRADLEY, FORMER NBA BASKETBALL
PLAYER AND UNITED STATES SENATOR

Starting a new business is hard work, possibly the hardest thing you'll ever do. It involves long hours and hearing "no" more times than you can imagine. You're going to need some pretty major motivation to get through the tough times, the loneliness, and the challenge of keeping your team and yourself moving forward.

MOTIVATION AND PASSION

Before you get started, it's important to understand and

articulate WHY you want to start a business. There are a ton of great reasons to found a company, and a few not so good ones.

- I want more control over my work.
- I love to build things.
- I need to create a solution to a big problem I have or see.
- I invented something that people will want.
- I think I can be a great startup leader.
- I have been an employee in startups and it's my turn to found something.
- My friends/colleagues want to work together.
- I want passive income.
- I want more income.
- I want to build a legacy for my family.
- I have a great idea and I want to get it out to the world.
- I want to get rich.
- I'm really passionate about XYZ.
- I hate my boss.
- I hate my company.
- If not now, then when?
- I don't want regrets later in life.

PASSION ISN'T ENOUGH

I'm not one of those people who'll tell you to simply follow your passion and the money will come. I love to cook and garden, but I'm not going to start a restaurant or landscaping business. My hobbies aren't where my businesses skills lie. There are many others who'll build great new restaurants and landscaping companies. Some businesses are best started by people who've had significant experience in those industries.

Being passionate about something doesn't mean you're good at it. Just watch a few seasons of *America's Got Talent, The Voice,* or *Last Comic Standing* and you'll see plenty of people who are passionate but not very talented.

But passion is crucially important in starting a business. You take the losses and the wins personally. Passion helps get you through the hard times. It is perhaps the strongest motivation. But passion and motivation aren't nearly enough.

You also need to do some research into the business part of your passion. How will a yoga studio attract and keep customers? How much does retail space cost? How much do you need to pay your instructors? How much will you need to invest to get it up and running? How much profit will there be and will it be enough to replicate your current income? This last question is crucial for you, the mid-life entrepreneur.

You want to find opportunities where your passions and talents intersect with market demand. Finally, you want to pursue a business where you can put your talents to work. The best ideas for *your business* will come where those intersect, like this:

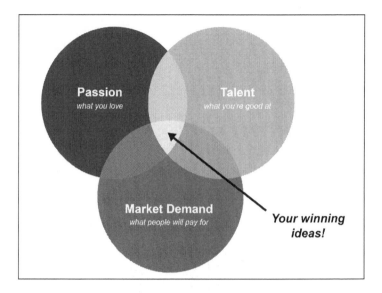

Passion
what you love

Talent
what you're good at

Market Demand
what people will pay for

Your winning ideas!

THE SCIENCE BEHIND MOTIVATION

One question you should ask yourself is: What motivates me the most? Is it positive motivation, like praise, money, or some other reward? Or negative motivation, like the avoidance of criticism or punishment?

You might think that we humans are motivated by natural instincts, that we're driven simply to satisfy our hunger for food or our desire for sexual pleasure. Humans do have these motivations, but thankfully we are more complex than that.

For a long time, psychologists believed that *incentives* were the driving factor motivating us. If you want employees to perform, you offer incentives. They can be positive incentives like bonuses or negative incentives like "improve your performance or you're fired."

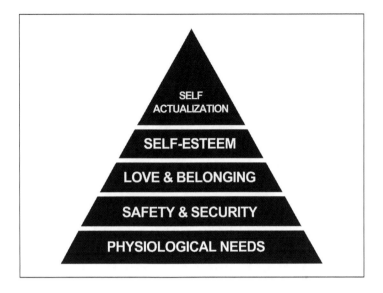

Many of you are probably familiar with psychologist Abraham Maslow's theory of the *hierarchy of needs*. Maslow believed that humans are motivated to fulfill certain "basic" needs before moving on to "growth" needs of a higher order. He depicted five motivational needs in a pyramid-shaped hierarchy and coined the term "metamotivation" to describe how people go beyond basic needs to strive for self-betterment.

MASLOW'S HIERARCHY OF NEEDS

The challenge with Maslow's framework for entrepreneurs is that "love/belonging" and "esteem" are very elusive for founders. Even if you are founding a company with your best friends, you probably aren't doing it for love and belonging. In fact, you will feel lonelier as a founder than you did as an employee.

Do you thrive on self-esteem or recognition? You're not likely to find much as a founder. There is no one to pat you on the back like a boss and no one to recognize your efforts.

But motivational theories didn't stop with Maslow. In the last fifty years, psychologists have been busy expanding on Maslow's incentives model, and they have found some models that work much better for entrepreneurs.

In his 2009 book *Drive: The Surprising Truth About What Motivates Us*, author Daniel Pink highlights studies that show how the old methods of motivation, the use of rewards and punishments, carrots and sticks, often produce worse outcomes.[7] As work has become more about creativity, the rewards of payment or the punishment of negative incentives apply less.

Sometimes we're motivated to solve challenging problems simply because it's fun or interesting. As it turns out, we're wired this way. Psychologist Harry Harlow found that monkeys would solve challenging puzzles that were simply left in their cages. There were no motivational rewards. The performance of the task was its own "intrinsic reward."

Pink created his own categories of motivations, isolating three factors that make work intrinsically motivating: *autonomy, mastery, and purpose*. In work environments that increasingly require creative skills to solve problems, these factors produce the highest outcomes.

All people need a degree of control in their work lives in order to feel motivated and fulfilled. The question is: Can a corporate job with its layers of management and top-down control help you find autonomy, mastery, and purpose? Corporate structures generally don't accept, acknowledge, or promote autonomy. They were set up in a "command and control" era. That old structure isn't conducive to producing brilliance or even creative thinking.

No one expects great artists to sit in an office cubicle and paint for eight and a half hours a day, or to be evaluated yearly by a supervisor for a meager 3 percent raise.

For you to be fulfilled, you need autonomy. And there is no more autonomous way to work than as an entrepreneur. You decide what to pursue. You decide where to work. You decide the goals and the method of attaining them. You take control, asserting your own mastery and purpose.

You might think that your primary motivation is money. Perhaps it is, but a desire to get rich isn't going to get you through a startup. Money isn't enough without a sense of purpose.

The path to becoming a successful entrepreneur is riddled with amazing highs and difficult lows. Just as you ready your product to ship, your lead developer tells you he's discovered a problem. The big sales deal you thought was in the bag goes to your competitor. Tech entrepreneur and author Ben Horowitz calls it "the struggle."

To get over the hard times, you'll need more incentive than just money. You'll need to feel the intrinsic rewards in the exercise of your own creativity and problem solving. You'll need to be continually cultivating your purpose, autonomy, and mastery.

THREE CRUCIAL QUESTIONS

As you prepare to embark on your journey of entrepreneurship, ask yourself three crucial questions:

WHY THIS IDEA?

What is it about your business idea that gets you excited? What market is there for it? Are customers likely to be as excited as you are?

WHY YOU?

What skills and experiences do you possess to make you the right founder for this company? What people can you attract to work at your company? Is your network tapped into customers, suppliers, or employees?

WHY NOW?

Why is this the right time to pursue your startup? Is now your time to seize the moment? Is the market ready for your product or service? Are you financially ready to pursue your idea full time or part time on the side?

Maybe you're like John Levisay, a former executive at GE and eBay and now founder of Craftsy, an online market for bringing creative pursuits to life:

I guess I always had the desire to be an entrepreneur, but I think I was somewhat methodical and realistic about what skills I would eventually need to do so effectively. You get to this point of "why not me?" And you begin to gain a little more confidence in your experience, perspective, and abilities.

KNOW YOUR BIG WHY

There is an even bigger *"why?"* that entrepreneurs need to answer for themselves. Tapping into the big *why* of your business is a crucial part of understanding and articulating your startup.

Simon Sinek, in his now-famous TED talk, suggests that few businesses understand their *why*.

Even more important than "what the business does" or "how the business does it," your *why* is your purpose, cause, and belief. Sinek paints a picture in which the *why* is at the center of everything the business does. Importantly, your *why* is not about making money or profit; those are only results.

There is a reason that Thomas Edison, one of the most prolific inventors of the modern era, said, "Genius is 1 percent inspiration, 99 percent perspiration."

All new projects run into bumpy patches. There will be times when you will question yourself. You will question your vision. You will question your skills. You will question your resolve. Your *why* will help you through it all. It can be both a push and a pull mechanism, pushing you to accomplish just one more small task and pulling you forward to the next one.

You might not be prepared to articulate the *why* of your business just yet but you should come to know it in your heart and mind. It's your company's *raison d'être*, its reason for being, your higher purpose in doing business. It's your theme song, like "Gonna Fly Now" (the theme song from *Rocky*) or perhaps an anthem by Eminem.

Sinek's TED talk was about articulating your *why* in order to tap into customer consciousness to appeal to consumer emotions, the way a company like Apple does.

Finding your own *why* is important in leadership both for yourself and your team. It's the only way I know of to power through difficult times. You'll need to keep your *why* handy and refer to it often.

Paul Graham, founder of successful incubator Y Combinator, once wrote a blog post called *How Not to Die*. In it, he noted:

> When startups die, the official cause of death is always either running out of money or a critical founder bailing. Often the two occur simultaneously. But I think the underlying cause is usually that they've become demoralized. You rarely hear of a startup that's working around the clock doing deals and pumping out new features and dies because they can't pay their bills and their ISP unplugs their server.
>
> Startups rarely die in mid keystroke. So keep typing![8]

When you know your *why*, your company's reason for being, your underlying and overriding purpose, you'll be less likely to become demoralized. Your *why* will sustain you and your staff through hard times. It will enable you to take heart and keep trying, rethinking and retooling as you go.

Think back to the questions I asked about your motivation. To cultivate your own *why*, try to discover your underlying motivations. For many entrepreneurs, it is a burning desire to bring their product idea to market. For others, it is a need to control their work.

One reason it's so important to get to the root of your motivations is that they will have a huge impact on the path you take to build your company, to raise funding, and to plan your "end game."

Now that we have spent time uncovering your motivations, let's take a look at some fears that might be holding you back and learn how to overcome them.

BEFORE YOU LEAP

"An essential aspect of creativity is not being afraid to fail. Scientists pursue a great invention by calling their activities hypotheses and experiments [and make] it permissible to fail repeatedly until in the end they get the results they want."

EDWIN LAND, FOUNDER, CEO, AND CHIEF
SCIENTIST OF POLAROID CORPORATION

Edwin Land was one of the most prolific inventors of our time. At Polaroid, he was renowned for his ability to persevere despite repeated failures. We think of Polaroid as a camera company, but Land held more than 500 patents in chemistry, polarization, military targeting systems, and many other fields. He had a healthy regard for failure as a learning process.

We all have fears to overcome when starting a new business.

This is especially true for older entrepreneurs. You have more to lose, including reputation, career momentum, and money. You have more responsibilities and demands on your time and resources.

Most of the founders I interviewed for this book had genuine fears to overcome. The most common were fears of failure and the unknown. Another that was quite common was the fear of not really knowing what you're doing. Many founders had been successful running departments, growing other people's companies, navigating corporate jobs, and rising up the ladder, but starting their own business venture was another thing entirely. More was at risk personally, professionally, and financially.

ARE MY FEARS REAL?

When I started my first company, I felt those fears viscerally. I hadn't felt like that before. Fear is one of the most debilitating emotions that any entrepreneur will face. It can freeze you in your tracks. My wife came up with a little trick to help me through this:

On a particularly bad day she asked me, "Did you quit?"

I told her no.

"Did you move the ball down the field?"

"Yes," I said, with clear frustration, "about an inch."

"Great," she said, "that inch is progress."

Forward motion in small increments counts on the field and it counts some days as an entrepreneur. If you're concerned about your investment, start small. If you're concerned about the market, prove your idea in baby steps. Test your idea at night or on days off. You don't need to quit your job *yet*. Get your business idea moving, contact prospective customers, and prove the value first. It will lower your risk substantially.

At the same time, seek out mentors who can help you through rough patches with practical advice borne of experience. Consider working with cofounders, perhaps informally at first. This will lower your risk while providing validation of your enterprise. Shared risk and good company never hurt.

Something else to consider is whether your doubts and worries are based in fact. How rational are those fears?

Consider this: your corporate or other job might be more fragile than you think. Recent economic times have shown that layoffs can be plentiful and often not foreseen. How secure is your day job, anyway?

My job was eliminated when my company had a CEO change and the new leader wanted his own people. Even big, supposedly "stable" companies go through layoffs and restructurings.

For me, I needed a bit of a financial and emotional safety net before I was ready to start something of my own. I saved enough to be able to pursue my own business at a lower salary. I also joined up with cofounders I believed in. (Turns out not to have been a good match, but that's another story.) I was in a good place with my family. I had support.

Someone once said, "Leap and the net will appear." I think there's some truth to that, but I also think you can alleviate the risk of the leap by taking small steps to prepare yourself. Do your research, as I'll show you in Chapter 6. Think through the options and possible outcomes and then take action. As you start building your business, you'll also be building your own safety net. You can stair-step your way to becoming an entrepreneur, building methodically and assessing risk along the way.

Of course, you might be facing an entirely different type of fear—the fear of regret.

What if I don't start a company? What will my work life be like in five or ten years? What if I don't take control of my professional and financial life?

I certainly faced these fears, too. So did Kelly Cooper. Cooper spent decades at clothing companies J. Jill, Athleta, and retail giant Gap. She is now Chief Merchandising Officer of QOR, a hot new men's athletic clothing brand. According to Cooper:

> I guess there is a tipping point in your life when you say, "I'm too old to do a startup—no, wait, this is the right time to do a startup because I need to do it before it's too late!" The timing really factored into my decision. My gut was that it was the perfect time for me to roll the dice.

> Yes, I could have progressed through my career at the Gap and

happily retired at whatever age. But one, that's not interesting enough; two, the thought of creating something from scratch is an unbelievable opportunity; and three, having control over my own reward was super-enticing. So, it's such a funny feeling, like, "Should I just settle in and do the status quo, or should I stick my neck out and do something that's really scary?" I feel like sometimes I'm jumping into an ocean full of sharks, and it feels amazing.

SWIMMING WITH THE SHARKS OF UNCERTAINTY

Founding and growing a startup might be one of the hardest things you'll ever do. The amount of uncertainty can be crippling. Founders frequently feel overwhelmed. There are more hugely important "mission critical" tasks than there are hours in the day.

In most businesses, including almost all you've worked in before, uncertainty has bounds. Most companies serve known customers with existing products. Even if your job was to dream up and develop new products, you were still trying to build something for existing customers. You had established relationships. You were part of a team, and the organization had the support of finance, marketing, and other departments.

In startups, virtually everything is unbounded and unknown. Which customers are going to like your product? How do you write a press release? How do you hire a salesperson?

You will experience the most intensive learning you have ever known. Most of it will come from doing things wrong the first time, and perhaps a second time. You'll fail repeatedly, hopefully in small ways, but sometimes in large ways, as you test your idea on the market. The amount of failure, learning, repeatedly picking up yourself and your team, dusting yourself off, and trying again will make you want to quit.

Serial entrepreneur and former CEO of Twitter, Dick Costolo, put it this way: "There are *always* points in the startup's life when things are going very, very badly, and the stress can be unbearable. Knowing how to pick yourself up, and pick your team up, from those times is key."[9]

Ben Horowitz, founder and CEO of Loudcloud and Silicon Valley venture capital firm Andreessen Horowitz, wrote a very powerful blog post about the difficulty of managing your psychology as you steer the ship. He noted:

> Even if you know what you are doing, things go wrong. Things go wrong, because building a multifaceted human organization to compete and win in a dynamic, highly competitive market turns out to be really hard. If CEOs were graded on a curve, the mean on the test would be 22 out of a 100. This kind of mean can be psychologically challenging for a straight-A student. It is particularly challenging, because nobody tells you that the mean is 22.
>
> Nonetheless, very few people talk about it and I have never read anything on the topic. It's like the fight club of management: The first rule of the CEO psychological meltdown is, don't talk about the psychological meltdown.[10]

So how do you get through the psychological meltdown? I don't mean clinical depression, which is a bigger issue. CEO depression is also very real, the ups and downs of being a first-time entrepreneur—that feeling of "what should I do? I don't know what I'm doing and it's weighing on me."

You'll need to change your mindset from "win or lose" to "learn and keep trying" because every day will have small setbacks—and yes, small wins, too. Understand it all as a process and continue to persevere. Keep learning always—from this book, from the founders I've interviewed, and from their books as well. In these pages, I'll introduce you to the numerous resources available to new entrepreneurs, all of which will make your job easier.

CONSTRAINTS: WHAT CONSTRAINTS?

In addition to overcoming your fears, you should recognize that starting a company in mid-life does bring some real constraints. Experience is an advantage, but with age come responsibilities. You have demands on your time, family concerns, a mortgage, loan payments, and so much more.

You should be honest about your constraints so you can face them head on and manage them. If you don't, they can jump out and surprise you.

The most common constraints for mid-life founders are time, energy, family, money (also a possible asset), and our own perceptions.

For most of us in our forties (or older), we have a family, kids, a home (and the large mortgage payment that goes with it), and many interests and responsibilities that compete for our time and money.

I've found from my own experience and the experience of other entrepreneurs that constraints are easy to control and overcome when managed right.

You don't need a big pool of capital to start a company. You don't need to devote yourself night and day at the very beginning. Plenty of great businesses are started as "side gigs" while the founder kept his day job.

As you'll see from the stories of founders I've interviewed, constraints don't have to get in the way of your business and life goals.

For example, many of the entrepreneurs I spoke with talked upfront with their spouses about their startup and their concerns about the stresses it might put on the family. Many mid-life entrepreneurs design their day so that they can be home for dinner, help out with homework, or put the kids to bed. They manage the balance of startup life and family life. I have devoted an entire chapter to the challenges of managing this balance.

Perhaps two of the most difficult constraints are energy level and age perception. For most of us, our level of energy for dedicated, long bursts of work is lower now than it was when we were in our teens or twenties. I know mine is. I used to have a job where I regularly worked until midnight or even pulled all-nighters. I could never do that now. Twenty-something founders can and will do that, so if you're building a tech company or in a sector where you'll be competing with them, you will have to simply be smarter and more efficient.

It's not always a case where the company that works the longest hours wins. You can be more focused in planning your efforts and more accurate in doing the right things and not wasting as much time. You also can and will draw energy and motivation from your other interests and from the time you spend with your family.

Perception is another constraint. Younger founders will find a supportive group of friends, family, professors, and others. When you tell everyone you're starting a company, you might not find that same support at first. Many of your friends and family might focus on the risks in a way that they wouldn't for a twenty-something founder.

If you go to raise outside capital, you almost certainly will face a bias of venture capitalists for younger founders. Why? Because most venture capitalists and bankers tend to look for investments that look like the last big success, which in this case looks like a founder of Facebook or Airbnb. We'll cover fundraising in much more detail in Chapter 10.

The bottom line is that you can overcome all of these constraints. I will show you how through example after example of mid-life founders who've done just that.

YOUR TIME

There is nothing more valuable than your time. This is true in general and all the more true for mid-life entrepreneurs. In addition to your startup, you probably have a full time job, a spouse, and a family. You already have many demands on your time.

I've faced the same demands. As a founder, I always felt like, *Which super-important thing should I do, and which should I not do yet?*

I wrote this book and launched a blog in my mornings and weekends while working a full time job. I coach my kids in sports and volunteer at Scouts. How do I fit it all in?

The answer is "brutal prioritization." When setting priorities, ask yourself, "Will this really advance my business? Is it *the* most important thing I can do for my company?" Questions like these are pretty effective for scratching things off your list that might not be the most important or efficient.

YOUR MONEY

Money is a double-edged sword for a mid-life entrepreneur. On the one hand, you probably have some savings or even quite a bit amassed from your decades of working. On the other hand, you have the many expenses of adult life: a mortgage, family, kids, insurance, saving for retirement. The list goes on and on.

Your natural instinct might be to save aggressively in

preparation for leaving your job and working full time on your startup. Certainly many financial experts will tell you to do just that.

I think about it a little differently. Sure, saving to prepare is fine, but don't overdo it. Consider taking a bit of extra money and *investing* it in your startup. Spend some money on Google AdWords or Facebook advertising and start building an e-mail list. If you'll be selling a product, prepare by producing some inventory in advance. Get professional business cards. Attend networking events. Hire a virtual administrator (VA).

Obviously, you don't want to go crazy here and waste tons of money. But small investments to get your business moving faster and generating more revenue—such as building your network, getting good legal counsel, or patent protection—will set the stage for your business to be viable and support you and your dreams. These are good investments.

AGE: LIABILITY OR ASSET?

Your work experience and life experience have given you a very large pool of assets to use to build your new business. Most people hear the word "assets" and think only of money—financial assets like stocks, bonds, home equity, or savings.

But personal skills, life experiences, your network, and your mindset are also assets you need and already possess. Whether you've started a company earlier in your career or not, you've spent decades acquiring work skills and personal skills.

Think about those skills and what you know now compared to what you knew 25 years ago. It's night and day, right? Over time you've acquired critical skills for launching any successful new business. You're in a better position now with those highly developed skills than many younger entrepreneurs.

Your personal traits have also likely improved as you've moved through life. One of the most important of these is perseverance.

Anyone who had to find a job during the recession of 1991 like I did or lived through the tech bubble bursting in 2001 or the Great Recession in 2008 has developed a very strong capacity to hustle and persevere. Your perseverance might have also been tested and developed outside of the professional realm with family or health challenges.

It's like steel coming out of a foundry—the harder it gets pounded, the tougher the steel is.

As Steve Jobs of Apple once said, "I'm convinced that about half of what separates the successful entrepreneurs from the non-successful ones is pure perseverance."

GET HAPPY WITH THE JOURNEY

Creating a company isn't about a destination. You want to control your work, to feel a sense of purpose, and to create income and wealth. There's no magical Nirvana of having "made it" in the end. It's a process and a journey, the ongoing business of doing business.

The hardest part of being a founder is getting happy with uncertainty. You'll need to maintain your focus on your product or service, your higher purpose, your big *why*.

In this new journey you'll encounter people who won't understand what you're about. These naysayers probably won't come right out and say, "You can't do it." They'll be subtler: "You started a company—are you aware of the risk?" or "Wow, what are you going to do if it doesn't work?" or "How do Karen and the kids feel about you taking on all that risk?"

You can dismiss the negativity in the beginning when you're full of enthusiasm. It gets a lot harder when you're nine months in and customers aren't as excited as you are. Or you're a few years in and finally determine you need to change direction—or "pivot," in startup lingo. Then it becomes easier to listen to those naysayers. Don't. Keep to your tasks and focus on your big *why*. Remember Thomas Edison: 1 percent inspiration, 99 percent perspiration.

Have you noticed that some people just seem to get a lot done on the job? They don't need a huge amount of management oversight. They don't whine much and they figure out how to overcome obstacles. The best founders and startup staff have that internal drive. As one blogger put it, they are "battery powered."

You're going to need this kind of drive for your business. Nothing is as infectious as positive energy.

GETTING ON YOUR WAY

You know your fears, your concerns, and your constraints. You know your assets and advantages. You've given considerable thought to the three crucial questions: *Why this idea? Why you? Why now?*

You've thought through and defined your big *why*—the overriding purpose, cause, and belief that drives you and your business to succeed.

You want to take control. You're ready to take the plunge or you're gearing up to do it. You're almost there, but there's still more you want to know. Starting a business in the world today is not uncharted territory. Many have gone before you, and on the following pages we'll be talking with some of the best who'll help show the way.

WHAT YOU BRING
TO THE TABLE

*"Do not let what you cannot do
interfere with what you can do."*

JOHN WOODEN, COLLEGE BASKETBALL COACH

As I just highlighted, this is an incredible time to start a new business and begin taking control of your work and your wealth. It is also a fantastic time based on the skills and experience you have accumulated over twenty-plus years of work and life. In this chapter, we will get into what you bring to the table as a mid-life founder. It's substantial.

One of the most common reasons that mid-career professionals wait to start a company is to further develop their business skills. Being a founder and CEO means assuming responsibility for every aspect of a company, and it requires a breadth of skills that very few young founders possess. While it is possible to acquire these skills while growing your own company, it's a challenge.

There is no ideal path to becoming a founder and CEO. Founders come from marketing, sales, finance, product development, even customer support. Having a diverse background is probably best because it means you have some base-level knowledge and understanding in many of the critical functions necessary for growing a successful business.

On the other hand, founders who have risen in their careers through the mastery of a particular skill set, like marketing or product development, find plenty of cross-over to other functions. People who've run marketing teams gain some familiarity with sales, finance, legal, and many other functions.

The broader and deeper a founder's core competencies, the better it is for the company.

John Levisay spent fifteen years at companies like General Electric and eBay developing his skills and confidence before becoming an entrepreneur. He told me:

> I guess I always had the desire to be an entrepreneur, but I think I was somewhat methodical and realistic about what skills I would eventually need to do so effectively... I came out of undergrad with a liberal arts major, and I knew what I needed [to learn] in order to really run a scale operation...so I went to General Electric and was in their training program in finance and accounting where they rotate you to different businesses. I spent about five

years at GE, and then decided to go back to school to kind of round out further and got my MBA.

So I ended up going into banking for two years after my MBA. But that's where I felt...there wasn't a great deal of learning. I was applying a lot of the things I'd learned, but I wasn't continuing to expand my market basket of skills, particularly [because] banking is very transactional.

I wasn't building something, so in 1999 I went to eBay when it was still a relatively young company and [I] saw that growth. From '99 to 2006...I saw all the successes but also all the traps, where you can gain this functional [expertise. But it was also] very tribal [in terms of] silos evolving within eBay. And in many ways, by the end of my career at eBay, it [had] evolved [into] bureaucracies often more complicated than established companies.

[That's] when I really got the bug, and at that point I had experience in finance and accounting, strategy, business development, and marketing. And I began to feel that I had the perspective and the experience. And seeing a fast-growth company, I got to the point where I said, "I can do this." At the point when I left eBay, I was probably in my late thirties.

I asked Levisay more about getting to that place where he felt ready to venture out on his own:

Kornblum: You didn't have that level of confidence before your late thirties?

Levisay: I don't think so, [although] maybe some of it was

humility, [but] I don't think I had [sufficient] experience. I didn't know enough.

Kornblum: Did you manage a team at eBay? Was that part of your learning curve?

Levisay: I did. I managed one of our acquisitions, which was about 100 employees... There was a mass exodus from eBay in 2005/2006, and that's when you get old enough [and] you start to see people you know running companies... Then a light kind of went on—*Oh wow, they're not smarter than I am.*

Kornblum: You felt, "I can do that, too."

Levisay: Right. You get to this point of "why not me"? And you begin to gain a little more confidence in your experience, perspective, and abilities. [I] had another job or two, [still trying to] figure out what was next, and then at about age 42 decided it was time.

YOUR MANAGERIAL SKILLS

In addition to developing functional skills, many mid-life entrepreneurs defer founding in order to develop their managerial skills, just as Levisay did. Managerial experience gives them an advantage over less experienced, younger founders in organizing the many tasks of getting a new company off the ground.

As a founder, you'll call on every aspect of your managerial experience. You'll need to attract, hire, and guide people.

You'll need to plan and manage projects. You'll need to know how to pitch in without micromanaging, and how to set direction, then leave the team alone to produce. You'll need to make executive decisions by weighing all the known facts and opinions from your various team members and other constituents such as investors and customers.

Over your decades of working, you've likely been part of some great workplace teams and some not so great ones. From the great ones you've learned how to put together a project plan and to make sure everyone on the team knows their role, goals, and timelines. Startups often feel like a series of small, concurrent projects. Keeping them all in line is part of the CEO's job.

YOUR SELLING SAVVY

The ability to sell is absolutely critical for any new business. As a mid-life entrepreneur, you've likely sold directly for a company or had to present and sell your ideas, yourself, or your projects. If you have presented your ideas to a group or tried to convince a job candidate to join your company, you were selling. Many people believe selling can feel "pushy" or "slick."

You shouldn't start a business thinking someone else will do the selling. Founders sell, especially in the beginning. Customers want to speak with the founder or CEO to get a sense of who is behind the product. You don't need to be slick. You just need to listen to their problems, present your product or service as the solution, and listen to their issues once they buy.

In addition to directly selling to customers, you will have to sell the vision of your new business to new employees, to partners, and to investors.

YOUR RECRUITING SKILLS

An offshoot of selling is recruiting. New companies are only as good as the team that builds them, so you need to be able to recruit. You are selling the vision, the opportunity, the passion, the dream, and your *why* to a prospective employee. Don't think of recruiting as an HR function. Most of your first employees will come to work for your startup because of you and your vision.

If you're building a high-growth business, then you need to be able to hire folks in critical path areas quickly. If you're starting a technology-based company, you need to be able to hire engineers or it will limit your ability to get products completed and shipped. If you're starting a design-heavy company, or a manufacturing-heavy company, then you will need designers or manufacturing experts.

Founders often choose to start their companies with a group of cofounders who are roughly in sync. You might also need to recruit crucial hires who are not cofounders. In most cases there will be at least a few critical people in special functions you'll need to bring on board.

Sometimes those critical people are right under your nose at your present job. That's what Sara Schaer, founder of the mobile app KangaDo, found out. Schaer had been a very successful product manager at Snapfish and at Hewlett Packard.

When she started KangaDo to help parents navigate the challenge of childcare and transportation, she asked former colleagues about her ideas.

I would say there was one other thing that kind of nudged me over the edge, and that was when my engineering [peer] who worked with me at Snapfish.com also left the company about the same time that I did. [He] came to me one day and said, "So, what are we doing? Seriously, what are we doing?" This is one of the most brilliant engineers in the Valley asking me, "What are we doing?"

I'm thinking, *I should share my idea with him and maybe he'll shoot it down. I don't know what he thinks. He could work anywhere with his skills.* So I sent him the few ideas I had and I didn't hear back for a few days, and then I called him up and said, "Well, what did you think?" totally expecting to hear, "Yeah, well, no thanks. I'm going to work at Google."

In fact, the answer I got was, "Hey, this looks cool. Looks like a product to me. I started coding it." And so I said, "Whoa, whoa, we have to take a step back here before we start coding anything. But seriously? You're really up for this?" He said "Yes, absolutely, I'm up for this."

And I should say the first next step that we took after fleshing the idea out for a month or two and doing more research was to reach out to some of the fantastic designers that we had worked together with at Snapfish. [We] didn't expect to get a "yes" from them, either, but when we told them what we were up to, they said, "Oh, count us in! We'll work for free, we'll moonlight. You know, absolutely, this sounds cool!" So we kind of magically had a team of superb professionals...experienced [people] came together with no need for a lot of resources at that point.

You might or might not want cofounders. We explore the pros and cons of cofounders more deeply in Chapter 7. In any case, you'll need to know where to turn for assistance. You should have mentors and advisors who can guide you in marketing and product development. You should absolutely have some folks you can call for moral support, other than your spouse and cofounders. Especially in the early days, meet regularly with your advisors and mentors.

YOUR LEADERSHIP ABILITY

The most important professional skill you've developed, and your overwhelming advantage over young founders, is leadership. Leading teams of people is often the most crucial skill a founder will use. In getting your new company going, you are actually willing it to life with dozens of different work streams that need direction and leadership.

Great leaders give a team focus. They motivate by sheer personality and deep inner bearing. They can get a team to go the extra mile and will guide staff through difficult times.

Leadership is coupled with confidence or "presence," the ability to project self-assurance and poise. Mid-life founders with business experience bring that presence to their leadership. It's a confidence born of innumerable business situations, deal-making, and applied skills.

Knowing how to approach a sales meeting with a new customer, knowing how to recruit a new team member, or knowing how to recover from a seemingly critical blow all get better with age. That kind of confidence is earned and internalized over time. It's the ability to convey to others, "Yeah, we got this."

YOUR PRESENTATION SKILLS

The ability to present your idea, product, or service might be one of the most powerful skills you've developed. As a founder, you'll need to make formal and informal presentations with some frequency.

Company leaders pitch investors, make sales to customers, unveil new products, present the state of the company, develop new partnerships, and "sell" their enthusiasm constantly.

In the course of your work life, you've likely developed the ability to organize and thoughtfully present your ideas. Even if public speaking makes you nervous, you probably already have a number of PowerPoint presentations under your belt. As a founder, CEO, and leader of your new business, you'll need to continually refine and improve your presentation skills.

YOUR ABILITY TO PRIORITIZE

Part of the challenge of finding balance in a new business is the seemingly endless list of tasks. In order to get it all done, you have to prioritize. The art of managing priorities in a startup is quite different, however, than managing in a corporate environment.

Prioritizing in a startup involves not only figuring out the order of doing things but what *not* to do. I call this the "not-do" list, and it is one of the most crucial parts of startup management, especially in a one-person company.

According to the legendary Steve Jobs, "People think focus means saying yes to the thing you've got to focus on. But that's not what it means at all. It means saying no to the hundred other good ideas that there are. You have to pick carefully. I'm actually as proud of the things we haven't done as the things I have done. Innovation is saying no to 1,000 things."

Prioritizing enables you to reduce your seemingly endless days to manageable ones. How many projects can your company take on *right now*? Who is going to do them? What are the goals? In my experience, small companies can handle three initiatives at any point in time, maybe five at most. So if your company's to-do list is too long, you and your people will be struggling to get it all done.

If you're a "solopreneur" or a "lifestyle entrepreneur" focused more on personal rewards than profit, the need to prioritize is even greater because everything falls on you. Part of the reason you started a business might be the freedom to set your own hours and quality of life. How do you attain that?

In my conversation with Craftsy founder John Levisay, he addressed time constraints, the value of managerial experience, and prioritization:

> When you have professional maturity, you're focused and can

say no to opportunities...[that] could overwhelm the business. Being able to say no to things and focus the team on no more than three to five critical success factors is key... We make a list... at the beginning of the year and every quarter of the things we are going to work on and, more importantly, things we're not going to work on.

And that is where I think a lot of young entrepreneurs that I've seen get in trouble... [They] underestimate the amount of work it takes to do something right. The fact that all of our founders have worked an average of fifteen years generally [means] there is a focus and a roadmap.

We all had young children, with the exception of one, [so] it forces focus. You can't be sitting around the office until two or three in the morning on a consistent basis. [With] young founders...there is a lot of socializing...because you know you are going to be at the office until midnight. Knowing you've got to be home a couple days a week at 8:00, it drives focus.

That doesn't mean you don't plug back in later [in the day]. But when you are thinking about [certain] elements of the business, there's a diminishing return to hours spent.

Part of learning to be an entrepreneur is learning to approach tasks with a "just get it done" approach. The perfectionist in you might not like it, but the old saying "perfect is the enemy of good" is right on. In a new business, it's more like "perfect is the enemy of done." Get it done and off your list. If it needs improvement, you'll know soon enough and can come back to it.

Stephen Covey, author of *The 7 Habits of Highly Effective People*, noted that United States president and military leader Dwight Eisenhower used to break tasks down to two dimensions: important and urgent. In a startup it will feel like everything is urgent, but try to keep focused on the important stuff.

Concept from Stephen Covey, *The 7 Habits of Highly Effective People*

To balance all of your competing priorities, you might need to give up some things for a short time. As a new mid-life entrepreneur, you'll feel like you have more than a million things to accomplish. Even if you've been able to quit your day job to devote yourself full time to your startup, you'll still have other commitments, including family.

As Oprah Winfrey once said, "You can have it all. Just not all at once."

So you might not be able to coach soccer, do your regular poker night or book club, take a vacation, or do any number of other things. You'll need to manage your endless "to-do" list.

What are the most important items to focus on? At the top of your list is interacting with customers, your network of mentors and advisors, cofounders, employees, and contractors. The most important priority is to prove the idea is a good one with customers.

If you are in a full time job, you'll need to decide how much time to set aside to work on your new business. This is where you need to be highly disciplined in scheduling. What goals will you set for the day, the week, the month? Schedule your time so you can hold yourself accountable to deadlines. If you don't, it's way too easy to blow off a task. Prioritize your goals.

If you start to see traction in your startup, you'll need to make those nights and weekends count. I'm not saying drop everything, but you'll need to make some tradeoffs. Your time is your most valuable resource right now, so use it wisely.

If you find yourself getting stuck, as many of us do, just try to keep things moving. You can get yourself unstuck by focusing on the next step and your next priority. Break down the problem, write it out, and use baby steps to get yourself moving again. Everyone gets stuck. It is such a common issue that I have devoted Chapter 13 entirely to getting unstuck.

YOUR PLANNING SKILLS

One of the great things about having a few decades of experience is that you've done planning before. Your planning skills are probably pretty sharp, which is one of the most important distinctions between younger and older entrepreneurs.

You'd be amazed at the lack of basic planning skills among young entrepreneurs. In a ten-week summer session I coached for a group of student entrepreneurs, few knew even the rudiments of planning ten weeks ahead.

You do not suffer those limitations. You have planned work projects, launched new initiatives, brought new products to market, planned and executed marketing campaigns, and created plans with Gantt charts or other tracking mechanisms.

Experience says you can't know where a project or initiative is going without a plan. Yet there are two critical differences to consider when planning a startup:

First, you have huge uncertainties about many of the assumptions going into the plan. In a big company, you know your resources. You know how much you have to spend on major items. You know how much each person will get done. In a startup, the variables are often unknown. So you will need to learn to plan with those unknowns.

The second major difference is that everything in a startup changes frequently. Your plans for the product will change because customers won't like certain features. Your plans for marketing will change because the copy or images won't work as expected. You will lose key team members at unfortunate times. So *re-planning* is one of the key skills for startup managers because startups are roller coasters.

YOUR ABILITY TO DELEGATE

You can probably delegate 10 to 20 percent of your workload right now.

As a founder, it's natural to feel the buck stops with you, because it does. Investors are backing you and so you feel the pressure to get everything done to build an enduring company. That feeling, however, can cause you to hang onto tasks that should be delegated to others.

Delegating tasks to either full time or contract staff enables you to focus on higher-level responsibilities more essential to the success of the business.

Early in my startup I felt compelled to constantly know where my company's money was going, so I personally managed the Quickbook accounts and expense reports, wrote all the checks, and took care of all financial matters. It was work I should have outsourced to a professional bookkeeper and saved myself the time. Now I know better.

Even if you're a lifestyle entrepreneur not looking for financial profit in your startup, finding a few great contractors to handle website development, online marketing, or even administrative tasks can relieve you of a huge time sink. If you're not sure how to find the right contractors, ask around and read reviews.

Remember why you started your business: freedom from a 9 to 5 job, freedom from a boss, and freedom to work when and where you want, for yourself and those you love.

YOUR FINANCIAL SKILLS

Cash flow is everything. Running out of cash means you cannot pay your employees and contractors. It means you can't order inventory for your store. It means you can't pay yourself.

You've survived for twenty years managing a household budget, paying rent or a mortgage, managing departmental budgeting at work, paying bills, saving some money. So you probably already have some basic financial skills.

It's also possible that you come out of marketing, sales, or customer support where your exposure to the financial aspects of companies has been limited. You might not be a "numbers person," but you don't need to be a spreadsheet jockey or CPA. You probably already know the basics of using, manipulating, and reading a spreadsheet.

Eventually you'll hire a controller and a chief financial officer, but until then it's up to you. First and foremost, the single most important question every startup CEO needs to answer is: *How much cash do we have and how long will it last?*

Going through the basics of a financial plan is one of the important steps in evaluating and testing your idea. You need to see if you can make a business of it. We'll delve more deeply into building a basic financial plan in Chapter 8. I also included a basic financial plan template as one of the bonuses for readers. You can visit www.nevertoolatetostartup.com/bonuses to access your bonuses.

YOUR BUDGETING KNOW-HOW

Another key skill that mid-life entrepreneurs bring to the table is budgeting. Having managed people and projects, as well as department and household budgets, you have a sense of how to put together some basic numbers. Still, you'll probably need the help of a contract bookkeeper or mentor, since your startup budget will probably be more complex.

Yet the overall concept is the same. You need to account for staff and other costs, and you need to have an understanding of cash flow. Even with a CFO or controller on board, the CEO is ultimately responsible for the company's numbers.

Unless you've hit it big in your corporate jobs or have some other sources of income, starting a company is going to be a pretty big financial burden. Even if you start your business on the side and begin producing revenue, it's not likely that you will entirely replace the income from your day job right away.

You'll probably need to take some preliminary steps to manage your spending, such as eliminating credit card debt, refinancing your mortgage while you still have regular paychecks, or swapping your expensive car for something more economical.

Many new founders mistakenly think they can raise money, quit their jobs, create their product or service, and start generating revenue at the get-go. It's unlikely, however, that you'll be able to raise outside capital for your company right away. You'll first need to test your idea, make some prototypes, and get feedback from potential customers. (We'll get more deeply into fundraising in Chapter 10.)

As you begin your startup, you'll need to be prepared to invest some small amounts in your company. Your investments should be ones that create value for the business, test your assumptions, and produce value for customers. Everything else is a waste at this early stage.

A good investment is anything that helps you get your idea to market quickly and helps grow your customer base, such as:

- Developing your website
- Hiring staff or contractors
- Prototype development
- Legal counsel

Other investments can wait, such as:

- Overhead, including rent, furniture, expensive computers, travel (unless it's to see prospective customers)
- Branding
- Expensive logos
- Market research studies
- Accountants

Your goal here is to invest in those things that increase your learning about your customer's need and your solution. Once you have those basics in place, you can focus your investment on scaling and growing your business as leanly and inexpensively as possible.

YOUR DECISION-MAKING SKILLS

One of the most important transitions you'll make as you move from employee to founder is your decision-making mindset. For some people, founding a startup is totally liberating. For others, it's a little intimidating. Personally I found both to be true. The decisions are all yours.

You get to control your work hours and location. You get to control what you work on. Want to get up at 10:00 and work until midnight? Do you love developing and designing products, but hate administration? No problem. You can hire out the admin work—just make sure someone does it.

It's your company, so go for it.

The hardest part of the transition might be realizing that the buck stops with you. The tough decisions are all on you. Your company's progress is on you. Too much to do? Sorry, it's on you to see it all gets done.

As an employee, you had a job with more narrow responsibility. As an entrepreneur, you will wear almost every hat. One day you're product management, the next you're tech support, the day after, you're sales. That can change hourly as well, not just daily. The life of an entrepreneur is filled with variety. You do whatever the business needs you to do.

The flip side of the coin is that no one stands in your way. No crappy boss, no corporate politics. That's all gone. You set the company culture. You control the direction and destiny of the business. You can build a small side gig that helps pay the bills, a freedom-producing cash-flow business, or a huge venture-backed company.

APPLYING YOUR SKILLS TO STARTUPS

A startup is not a small version of a big company. Until the startup has introduced a product that is well received in the marketplace, a startup is really a series of experiments. Founders are trying to see if their product or service resonates with prospective buyers/users, whether the business can attract customers in a profitable way, and whether their team members are compatible, all while trying to gauge market response.

It can be extremely helpful for a founder to have spent time in an early stage business before setting out to found his own. Working for a startup or small business can provide a much deeper understanding of what it is like to start a company and increases the likelihood of becoming a successful founder.

Startups operate differently than large companies by necessity. They make decisions very quickly and don't tend to have much process. In large companies, a hierarchy dictates what employees are able to contribute. In small businesses, employees are given much more freedom to contribute, often to the point of being asked to do things they've never done before. Someone has to do it, and startups have limited resources, so employees learn to do a lot more than their job title would suggest. They also learn to be highly resourceful. This freedom and pace of learning can be one of the attractions of working in a small business.

Noted founder and author Steve Blank puts it this way: "A startup is a temporary organization designed to search for a repeatable and scalable business model. A company is a permanent organization designed to execute a repeatable and scalable business model."

Because of the significant differences between startups and large companies, many would-be founders choose to get some experience in one or more startups as an employee or executive before founding their own company.

Tim Enwall, CEO of Revolv, which was acquired by Google Nest, had this to say about the learning curve in managing startups:

There's certainly lots of lessons learned that I did in the past that were successful that I'm repeating. How I empower the leaders who work for me is definitely a lesson I've learned. How we hire people is a lesson I've learned and getting that right and investing the time and doing that right—both of those are very important...

One of the most important things that you start to learn when you get older is you don't know all the answers, you're not perfect, you're not required to know all the answers and, therefore, having skilled resources around you—whether they're employees or contractors or advisors or whatever—is really critical.

So bringing those resources to bear...has been really important.

I like the challenge and I like the creativity and I like bringing people together. I think it's those three things. It is very difficult to create something that generates revenue and creates value and is sustainable, so I love challenges. You have to be very creative; it's constant...problem solving. I love bringing people together in the pursuit of something that's greater than what they could do by themselves.

Spending substantial time in one industry gives the founder a depth of understanding that is extremely helpful in growing a startup in the same or in a related industry. It can help a founder avoid huge, perhaps even fatal, mistakes in their own startup.

Kelly Cooper told me:

This is the sweet spot of my expertise. I've done it two times. I've taken two companies that weren't private label to private label. The difference [in founding QOR] is that there wasn't a company, there wasn't a brand already. In the other two instances there was volume and there was a brand, [but] in this instance there was literally nothing.

What the research says is that there is white space in men's athletic apparel. First of all, the men's athletic apparel industry is growing. More men are exercising, and men, older men, are exercising more and at a higher rate than younger men.

So what we're creating is a paradigm shift in the way men think about their clothes. We're introducing outdoor industry performance fabrics into more urban and street-wear styling.

Cooper had previous relationships with fabric suppliers and factories that enabled QOR to launch with a seventy-piece clothing line, more than five times larger than many other smaller clothing competitors.

> If I didn't have the relationships that I have with the fabric suppliers and the factories, I would never be able to do this. And that's [the] benefit, my value-add, versus a lot of people who are trying to do the same thing... I have these relationships and [I'm] calling in the favors based on my previous track record and that of my partners. If I didn't have the history, it would be very difficult. On the flip side, you would have to be crazy to do a clothing startup when you know as much as I do [about how hard it is]. I make 1,000 decisions every day. We scrutinize every detail—every button, every zipper, every stitch, every fabric, every measurement...every style, every day.

There are certain markets where previous industry experience can be crucial in understanding the nuances of customer problems and regulatory environments. If the founder and team do not possess that experience, they'll need to acquire it quickly. Any founder in a highly regulated industry, like health care, telecommunications, or transportation, will need to gain an understanding of the regulations and their impact on industry behavior.

It is not a requirement, however, to have experience in an industry. Many founders lack any experience in the industry they are entering. Ironically, that lack of experience helps them think differently or in new ways about their market. They approach things with a fresh perspective unencumbered by the way things are usually done. However, they have to balance the advantages of fresh thinking with the disadvantages of limited experience.

SKILL SHIFT

I have highlighted a number of times the incredible business and personal skills you already have that you can bring to your new business.

It would be overly simplistic, though, to suggest that you can simply drop your current skills onto your new startup and think you will be successful.

You need to adjust those skills to the new environment—the startup environment, where everything is more difficult. It is more difficult because you don't have the resources you are used to. It is more difficult because you are working under significantly more time pressure and with way less certainty about your assumptions.

A few examples:

- Sales: You bring tremendous sales skills from your corporate jobs. But in your new business, you are not working with the same brand that you did before. No one has heard of your new company. You also have no marketing budget, so instead of working on leads that a marketing department has brought in, you have to go develop leads yourself.

- Recruiting: You need to learn how to recruit with a limited budget, no brand, paying less than market, selling candidates on the incredible upside of equity and on the vision of the company you are building.
- Product development: In a big corporation, products are not released until they are done. Extensive market research often goes into gauging customer demand. In a startup, all of that is reversed. You build and ship an MVP (minimum viable product), get customer feedback on the MVP, and create new features on the fly. You might plan out a few weeks at a time, but rarely longer. Speed and iteration are everything.

Hopefully, you see now that you bring a depth and diversity of skills and experiences to your new business. These skills will improve your chances of entrepreneurial success. Now let's take a look at how to apply them to building your team and launching your business.

YOUR NETWORK IS KEY

As a mid-life entrepreneur, one of the largest assets you bring to bear is your network. Having worked for twenty years, you probably know experts in many functions and industries. You know prospective customers as well as people in production, design, and software.

Your network of business associates, colleagues, and friends is one of the most important leverage points for an entrepreneur. What do I mean by leverage? Advantage. Your network can help you in every way. Some people in your network will become your customers. Some will become cofounders or early employees. Some will become vendors or key contractors.

Your network also includes people who have started companies before, or who know a lot more about certain areas of your business than you do. Seek out these people as mentors, advisors, and guides. In some cases, these will be formal relationships where you meet regularly for business help. This is generally known as an "advisory board."

If you're contemplating starting a company, take the time to network in the local startup community. Find like-minded peers, a local accelerator or co-working space, or even a business school. Attend a few events and meet other entrepreneurs. They can help with referrals to any number of vetted service providers like CPAs, payroll processors, or insurance experts.

Being part of the community of startups can be critically important in helping the first-time CEO navigate. You will be amazed at how challenging it can be to be a new CEO, and how helpful it can be to have a sounding board and support network.

One of the many mistakes I made as a founder was that I did not use my network as effectively as I could have. It's not that I didn't have a great network. I did and still do, and I've learned to cultivate it pretty well. In the beginning, however, what I needed from my network was a support group. The emotional up-and-down journey of being a first-time founder was tough for me and I did not realize that essential fact until

I was well on my way. I also didn't use my network well for hiring employees.

In most cases, people in your network will help you learn or will guide you to others who can assist you. For instance, let's say you don't know much about online marketing. Someone in your network probably does, or they worked with a great agency on a project and can direct you to them. You'd be amazed by how much you can learn if you take someone to lunch.

With the assets and experience you bring to the table, you can manage your fears, your doubts, and the rough patches. With the advantage of your know-how, you're better equipped and primed to succeed. You are ready to get started on your entrepreneurial journey. In the next chapter, you will see why *now* is the right time.

THE BEST TIME IS NOW

---

*"It is a terrible thing, I think, in life, to wait
until you are ready. I have this feeling
now that actually no one is ever ready
to do anything. There is almost no such
thing as ready. There is only now. And
you may as well do it now. Generally
speaking, now is as good a time as any."*

HUGH LAURIE, ACTOR AND AUTHOR

Global factors and technology have coalesced to make *now* simply the best time in history to start a new business. This is driven by the power and reach of the Internet, by the forces of globalization, by the growth of software-as-a-service or just about anything-as-a-service, and by the explosion of training materials, how-tos, and user-generated content.

This does not mean you need to be an Internet or technology

entrepreneur. You don't need to be a techie or Internet whiz, the next Bill Gates or Mark Zuckerberg, to take advantage of the power of the Internet and the latest tools and trends.

You might want to start a tech or mobile app company, but perhaps your interests are simpler. Maybe you're starting a local business like a florist or tax preparer shop. It doesn't really matter what kind of business you want to start because the trends are in your favor.

What the Internet has done for all entrepreneurs is give them access to people, information, customers, tools, and support across the globe. All of this can be accessed through a browser. With a decent Internet connection, you can start, launch, and grow a new business from anywhere on the planet.

THE TREND IS YOUR FRIEND

There is an old expression from Wall Street stock traders that helps explain the power of positive or negative movements in stock prices: *"Don't fight the trend. The trend is your friend."*

What this means is that once a stock, or the market as a whole, starts moving in a certain direction, it is unlikely to reverse quickly. Traders generally don't want to bet against that movement.

The same is true for us as entrepreneurs. We need to be keenly aware of and be prepared to tap into today's trends in technology and the marketplace.

There were more than 3 billion Internet users in 2014, up from 35 million in 1995. Almost half of the people on earth are on the Internet.

Smartphone usage has grown even faster than Internet usage. In 2015, there were 5.2 billion mobile phone users, with 40 percent of those on smartphones.

Facebook, the ubiquitous community platform, has grown to more than 1.5 billion monthly active users in 2015. There is a lot more happening on Facebook than kitty pictures.

Google now processes more than 1.2 trillion searches a year. Yes, that's trillion.

These are some eye-popping numbers, but what do they mean for you?

They mean that access to incredible amounts of consumers and information has never been easier. The cost of launching a new business is dropping continuously as a result because you don't need to invest in infrastructure or hire employees.

It is all so much easier and cheaper. Venture capitalist Marc Andreessen, founder of Netscape and head of venture fund Andreessen Horowitz (www.a16z.com), has famously declared that "software is eating the world." He has also said, "With lower start-up costs and a vastly expanded market for online services, the result is a global economy that for the first time will be fully digitally wired."

You can get access to high-powered computing systems inexpensively, on a rent-as-you-go basis. You can also access the support that you need, in the form of software services, all of which are available in small component parts.

Stitching all of these services together used to require programmers or business analysts to make this run. However, the explosion of "application programming interfaces" or APIs, means that different services from different companies simply work together with little effort.

CONVERGING WAVES

As an entrepreneur, you sit in the middle of two great waves that are creating the best time in history to start a new business.

The first wave, the ability to reach billions of customers across the globe, enables you to find the specific customers you want without spending significant money on advertising.

The second wave, the vast amount of knowledge, support, and tools available online, allows you to test your idea and create your company inexpensively.

Both of these waves significantly lower your risk as a midlife entrepreneur.

As a result, the growth rates of new businesses and new ideas can be staggering. It used to be that a new business was happy to grow at 10 percent per year, and a "high growth" business was growing at 20 to 30 percent. Now, we see new

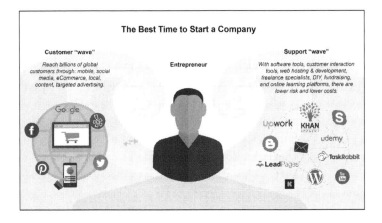

The Best Time to Start a Company

consumer-oriented businesses gaining millions of users in months. We see business-to-business, or B2B, startups growing at over 100 percent a year. We see viral growth of businesses that network people together.

We are seeing whole industries transformed by this growth. Here are some examples of businesses and industries transformed by new technologies:

OLD WAY	NEW WAY
Video rentals	Netflix
Hailing a cab	Uber or Lyft
Buying CDs	iTunes, Pandora, Spotify
Cash registers	Square
Telephones	Skype
Voicemail	Text messages, WhatsApp, Kik
Daily newspapers	Twitter
Retail stores	Amazon (and millions of other e-commerce sites)
Letters to the editor	Blogs
Publishing a book	Amazon Kindle self-publishing
Colleges (or professional certifications)	Online training and courses
Hiring employees	UpWork or Fiverr

The power is now in users' hands to consume information, publish thoughts, reach peers and communities, and use tools for lower cost with easy on/off access. Users are increasingly getting what they want, when they want it. This consumer power, coupled with mobile and Internet-based products and services, is creating extraordinary transformation of entire industries.

RESEARCHING YOUR MARKET

One of the great things about having easy access to billions of consumers and massive amounts of information is that you can research ideas for products and companies with little difficulty.

Start with Google. Search your business idea and see what already exists. Don't be dismayed if companies already offer your products or services. You have ways to make them better, or you should. In fact, it's helpful to know that other companies have already validated your market. You can copy their design, their marketing, use their suppliers, and innovate.

Yes, innovate. You should have some ideas about how your new business will be better than the existing companies.

In addition to being an amazing search engine, Google is also an incredible advertising platform, which has real value for you in market research. Advertisers run ads related to specific search terms. Google has some pretty powerful tools that will tell any prospective advertiser the number of searches for a particular word or phrase, and all of the related terms.

If you're not familiar with this tool, go to adwords.google.com/ KeywordPlanner. There you can create a free account and start your research. You'll find an incredible treasure trove of information on your likely consumers or business buyers. Are they looking for your product concepts or for related ideas? How frequently do people search for those terms?

Van Barker had been an executive in large companies like PepsiCo and Hewlett Packard before starting YardStash as a solution to storing his kids' bicycles. Barker used Google and Amazon in researching his new product:

> It was very much kind of a grassroots, guerrilla market research. But I will say, I think using the web was the primary method, just really going deep on searches for anything related to outdoor bicycle storage. And then, using a lot of spreadsheets, just kind of matching up price, features, so forth and so on.

> I did a lot of searching on market sizing. I used Amazon at times to look at product reviews, kind of triangulating the product sales ranking with other benchmarks to figure out how many were moving through the Amazon channel. And then a lot of it was just informal, since it was a product that I needed based on my neighborhood. There were a lot of my neighbors and friends who were in similar situations. So, a lot of qualitative, kind of back-and-forth with them. And then I also did a couple of surveys with local bicycle clubs. Just people I knew had hooked me up with their mailing list, through SurveyMonkey.

The basic idea here is to research *existing demand* for your product or service. If consumers are searching for something online, there is demand for it. If not, you'll be trying to *create demand* rather than fulfill demand. People search online for solutions to their problems. You know at least one method of reaching them: Google advertising.

The Internet won't be the full extent of your market research. It is, however, an incredible and free resource and tool for doing your preliminary research.

E-COMMERCE: THE POWER TO SELL DIRECT

In addition to finding and advertising to consumers online, you can also sell your products directly to online customers. Consumer expectations are changing. Increasingly, people do not want to get into their cars, drive to a mall, fight for parking, and wind their way through crowds to make an everyday purchase. They are buying online, driven by the ease of finding what they want, the increased speed of their broadband connection, the simplicity of ordering, and the speed of delivery to their front door. Consumers want to get what they want, when they want it, with ease and speed. This is an opportunity for you.

Starting in 1994 as an online bookstore, Amazon helped create the online shopping and e-commerce category. Steadily adding other products beyond books, Amazon has grown tremendously, producing almost $90 billion in revenue in 2014. Amazon has innovated along the way, introducing one-click ordering and its Prime membership two-day shipping service.

Amazon is certainly not the only show in town. Almost $800

billion will transact online through e-commerce in 2015. That amount is growing rapidly because of consumer demand. There is room for it to grow much further because e-commerce is still only 13 percent of total retail sales.[11]

As an entrepreneur, this creates significant opportunity for you, especially compared to the way things used to be.

Think about it. If you had a product to sell twenty years ago, you either opened your own store or approached various middlemen, such as distributors, to see if they could get it to retailers for you. Now you simply sell online directly to your customers.

Eric Bandholz left his corporate job as a financial advisor for Merrill Lynch to found Beardbrand, a men's grooming products company. According to Bandholz, "There wasn't anything out there for beardsmen who wanted a high-quality, premium product."[12]

So Bandholz started blogging about grooming techniques and made videos that he posted on YouTube, winning over a loyal following. With two other founders, they initially bootstrapped the business with fairly small sales.

Beardbrand got its big break when Bandholz was featured in a *New York Times* article and then an appearance on *Shark Tank*. Starting in a small category, using Internet search and social media to reach consumers, and selling online, Beardbrand did $450,000 a month in sales as of late 2014.

If you have a good idea with a unique and differentiated product or service, you can build your business through e-commerce. Entrepreneurs have built high-growth businesses in so many categories, including shoes (Zappos and ShoeBuy), razors (Harry's and Dollar Shave Club), Diapers (diapers.com), eyeglasses (Warby Parker), men's pants (Bonobos), curated clothing (Trunk Club for men, Stichfix for women), and many more.

In addition to physical products, digital products can be sold directly to customers via e-commerce. Consumer software is predominantly sold through download now, including productivity software like Evernote, antivirus software, online storage products like Dropbox, or online backup systems like Carbonite. Books, music, and games can all be sold directly to consumers.

One more recent trend in going direct through e-commerce is the sale of "information products." Webinars, e-books, e-mail how-tos, and video courses are all sold directly and are one of the best ways for bloggers to generate revenue. Writers can now earn a living by giving their audience direct access to their knowledge through an info product.

MICRO-MARKETING AND ADVERTISING

As few as ten or twenty years ago, starting a new business meant spending large sums of money on marketing to locate and find new customers. Most of the ways to market to customers were pretty inefficient and very expensive. Mass market advertising like TV, radio, and billboards cost tens of thousands of dollars to get started and millions to run at any scale, and their effectiveness was unclear. This was prohibitively expensive for most small businesses. It also was challenging because you had to spend money way ahead of getting customers.

There were some methods available to target specific audiences, like direct mail. However, direct mail has a very low response rate, 2 to 4 percent, which makes it tough to justify its cost, unless the product is expensive or a repeat purchase.

The Internet has largely changed that for businesses, enabling companies small and large to reach huge numbers of potential customers in their hometowns, across the country, and around the globe.

Advertising and targeting online can be inexpensive because Internet advertising enables you to reach a very specific audience for your new business. In other words, you don't need to cast your advertising dollars all over the place when you can target very specifically, which lowers the cost of reaching *your* customers. Equally important, you can track and analyze the effectiveness of Internet advertising, so you know what's working and what isn't.

The Internet now offers small businesses the ability to run extremely targeted advertising campaigns in what is called "micro-advertising," "micro-marketing," or "micro-targeting."

You can run campaigns on Google Adwords or Facebook for tens of dollars a day. You can also target these micro campaigns to very narrow segments of prospects. You can see which campaigns convert to customers, testing frequently, daily or even multiple times a day. This lets you be extremely efficient with your marketing dollars. If it works to produce customers, you keep it up. If not, you kill that campaign and start another.

Let's look at a few examples so you can see how micro-advertising isn't just for big brands like Apple or Ford.

We'll start with something obscure. Let's say you're a runner and you discover an amazing solution for plantar fasciitis. You decide to launch a new business selling your shoe insert for people with plantar fasciitis. Both Google and Facebook will enable you to advertise directly to consumers, but in different ways.

With Google, you can run ads based on what people search for. So you could run ads for people looking for "plantar fasciitis" or "fasciitis shoes" or "foot heel pain." You can do this for only dollars a day.

On Facebook it works quite differently. Facebook gathers so much detailed information about its users, like their location, their age, their sex, their family, and, most importantly, their interests and "likes." For instance, you could run ads to find middle-aged men who live in the United States who "like" the Dr. Scholl's brand.

Local businesses can also target and segment their advertising. The Internet enables you to find your local customers and advertise directly to them. And they also have an unprecedented ability to find you.

Directory and rating services like Yelp enable restaurants, gyms, and plenty of local business to get found. Google increasingly favors small and local companies in its search results. Groupon is a great way for a local business to generate initial awareness of a new establishment.

Advertisers clearly agree. Internet advertising is growing both in total dollars and in its share of all advertising. Over the last twenty years, Internet advertising grew to a whopping $14 billion in the first quarter of 2015 from virtually $0 in 1996.[13]

I don't advocate any of these business services in particular, but they are all worth investigating to get your message out.

KNOWLEDGE AT YOUR FINGERTIPS

As entrepreneurs, we are continually trying to learn the many different elements of running a business. In addition to obtaining a working understanding of your business, you also need to improve your leadership skills, your presentation skills, your fundraising and sales skills.

Getting that knowledge has never been as easy as it is now.

Knowledge and training today are only a click away. Free or very inexpensive courses are available online at sites like Udemy and Khan Academy, not to mention outstanding blogs that offer tips and advice. I am always amazed at the amount of free content available to guide me through setting up a website, doing payroll, creating a pivot table in Excel, or creating a venture capital pitch deck.

Most new businesses set up a website. You might not know how to build one yourself, so you think you'll need to hire someone to do it for you, right? Well, maybe not.

A quick search for "How to set up a website" reveals dozens of blogs with step-by-step instructions. If you're a visual learner, YouTube is a treasure trove of "how to" videos. You'll learn, for free, how to procure a domain name, hire a hosting company, buy and customize a theme, and obtain a logo. Presto, you have a new website for your business.

It's the same for setting up a blog, running an ad campaign on Google or Facebook, selling products through your website, or selling products on Amazon.

If it all still seems overwhelming after reading blog posts and viewing YouTube, you can simply take an online class to learn the ropes. You can also join online communities and Facebook peer groups comprised of individuals who'll support your learning. These can be great for troubleshooting as well. Inevitably you will run into challenges, and forums are great places to find help.

The bottom line is that learning is one of the most important entrepreneurial skills. With incredible information available at your fingers through your browser, learning has never been easier.

YOUR ONLINE TOOLS

If you've worked in larger companies, you might not be familiar with some of the online tools readily available for startups. They are usually easy to use and inexpensive to start with. I list some of these services below, but they aren't meant as endorsements—just a convenient way for you to get started investigating the possibilities.

Virtually all software you'd want to use for your small business is available in a software-as-a-service, or "SaaS," model, which enables you to pay monthly. You can use these pay-as-you-go software services for setting up your site, running ads, processing credit cards, and for payroll, e-commerce, even for keeping notes. You name it and it's most likely already available online, and in many cases for free.

Twenty years ago, setting up a website to showcase your business to prospective customers could cost thousands of dollars and required you to hire a web developer and a designer. You needed to hire someone to produce your logo and business cards. Setting up payroll required multiple meetings with payroll providers. Developing a newsletter for your existing customers meant finding a designer to do the layout, then a printing firm, then you or someone else to stuff envelopes and mail them out.

No matter what type of business you start, you will want a web presence. We used to have to pay designers and coders to set these up at a cost of thousands. Today, you can purchase your URL or domain name (the name of your site) from a registrar like GoDaddy. You can set up a professional-looking website using a publishing platform such as WordPress or a site-builder service like Wix.

You host your site either at your registrar or at a dedicated host like BlueHost, HostGator, or dozens of others. You pick a platform like WordPress to provide the basic plumbing and then you choose a theme, the visual look and feel of your site. Themes do a ton of the design work for you, and are modifiable with easy-to-use visual editor tools. And you can do it all for under $100.

Getting a logo for your new business is also easy on the Internet. You can get a basic logo done through Fiverr, a site where the most basic first-level tasks cost only $5. If you want something more professional, 99designs will create a design contest in which multiple designers submit logo concepts and you get to choose. These competitions cost as little as $299.

If you want to communicate with your customers through a blog on your site or through an e-mail newsletter, both are easy and inexpensive to set up. There are a number of great e-mail service providers like Constant Contact, MailChimp, AWeber, and others. You can start for free or for under $30 per month. These services offer professional-looking templates that integrate easily into your website and your visitors' e-mail.

One of the more amazing services to launch in the last few years is specialized webpages called "landing pages" dedicated to selling one particular product, service, or concept.

The creation of landing pages used to require knowledge of

programming and design. You had to know how to create and host the page, make it look attractive, and how to program actions such as e-mail capture, download, and purchase. Now you can use a service like LeadPages or Instapage that have templates for dozens of amazing landing pages with integrated services. You can host these pages on your own or hook them up easily to WordPress. It saves hundreds of hours and thousands of dollars.

Communicating with your team and your customers used to require setting up phone service for your startup and an e-mail server. Today you can use Skype, Gmail, and Google Voice. Skype is free and incredibly easy to set up and use. Gmail offers not only personal e-mail but business e-mail and costs only dollars a month per user. Google Voice allows you to create a phone number for your business with voicemail. That number will ring through to your mobile or any other phone you wish. Basically, you can set up a powerful communications platform for your startup in minutes that costs only dollars a month.

Once your business starts to grow, you will need to set up an accounting system. If you have hired employees, you'll have to pay them through a payroll system. You might even want to offer some level of benefits. There are great SaaS platforms for this as well.

For accounting, QuickBooks now offers a cloud-based system called QuickBooks Online. Or you can get something more sophisticated from vendors like NetSuite or Intacct. For payroll, there are lots of great services like Zenefits, ADP, and

Paychex. All of these are available through your browser for under $100 per month.

Honestly, there are so many great online services that it can be a little overwhelming. I've only mentioned a few. So ask around to see what services others are using. Depending on your needs, you can probably get started for as little as a few hundred dollars.

FINDING TALENT

Globalization is an incredibly powerful force in business today. Suppliers of products trade across borders regularly. Increasingly, the supply of labor is fluid as well. The same forces of globalization that we outlined earlier, the ones that can put your job at risk, can also be a boon to you as an entrepreneur.

Hundreds of millions of skilled workers are available for you to hire as freelancers with deep expertise to help you run your business. You can find them around the globe, from America, Europe, Asia, and South America.

Today you can find professional freelance talent for short-term or long-term projects for virtually every task under the sun, from marketing to sales, programming, design, accounting, writing, and much more.

Large marketplace Internet sites have exploded to help buyers and sellers of these kinds of services come together. Sites like UpWork (formerly oDesk), 99Designs, Fiverr, Task Rabbit, and many others enable the small business owner to find any professional he'd need.

It can be daunting at first to know who to hire, so the sites have ratings and reviews, and you can search by skills. These sites enable you to pay by credit card or PayPal so you don't have to manage overseas money transfers.

Another huge benefit is the management of regulatory paperwork. When you hire a contract worker in the United States, you have to file 1099 paperwork with the federal government. These sites manage all of that for you.

Whether you're trying to find low-cost experts to help on projects, or if your goal is to build a location-independent business with no permanent employees, freelancers and freelance marketplaces are one of the most powerful advances of the last twenty years.

The real power of this massive pool of freelance talent for you as an entrepreneur is that it lowers both your cost and your risk in hiring talent to start and grow your business. It lowers your cost because you only need to pay for the services you need. Rather than hire a full time programmer, you can hire a freelancer to do a week's work of coding. It lowers your risk because you don't need to worry as much about bad hires, and because you can keep your total overhead much lower.

COMMUNICATION REVOLUTION

The last twenty years have seen a total revolution in the way we communicate with people around the country and the globe. Long distance calling was paid for by the minute, and it was pretty expensive. International calling was really expensive. For new businesses, calling customers, suppliers, and vendors was pretty tough.

E-mail wasn't much better. Sure you could send lots of e-mails, but the back and forth was a challenge and deliverability was sometimes inconsistent.

Fast forward to today. Skype created the ability to use the Internet to call anyone and even include video, all for free. Google Hangouts has incorporated it into the Gmail system, so if you want to jump on a quick Skype to a software developer or marketer in Asia, you can do it super easily and for free.

Text messaging and other messaging platforms like Kik and WhatsApp have also given us the real-time aspect, all through our smartphones.

We also have more group-centric business messaging platforms like Slack and Salesforce Chatter. These let you create virtual rooms with permanent messages that can be reviewed, and with documents, tasks, and to-dos. Companies that adopt these platforms often see their e-mail traffic drop massively, since it is just a better way to communicate. Users seem to agree. Chatter has hundreds of thousands of users and Slack is one of the fastest growing B2B platforms ever, with over 1.1 million daily users.

Slack and Asana (my preference since it's a little more "to-do"-oriented) are also free to get started for small groups. These are a great way to communicate among your team, and free is a price every early stage founder loves.

SOURCING YOUR PRODUCTS

If your business involves selling physical products, you'll need a source for them. It used to be that finding a factory to produce products required specialized knowledge. You probably had to come from that industry and know someone who could make prototypes for you. It was an expensive and cumbersome process.

The combination of globalization and the Internet gives you the ability to find domestic or overseas factories. These factories can specialize in outsourced production. They produce prototypes or small-quantity production runs in a matter of weeks. Many of these are located in China although outsourced partners can be found in any part of the world, including South America, Eastern Europe, and other parts of Asia.

I'm not saying it's easy. There are a lot of challenges in finding the right factory, but it can be done with only clicks. The largest supplier website, Alibaba.com, has tens of thousands of Chinese factories listed, organized by specialty. The site lists information about each supplier, including their name and location, their minimum order sizes, turnaround times, and payment information. Importantly, it also includes ratings so that you can see which vendors are considered the best.

Payment is also relatively easy since many of these suppliers take PayPal. Alibaba also has its own secure payment system called Alipay.

CROWDFUNDING AND RAISING CAPITAL

Raising capital used to be extremely time consuming and expensive. You either had to know investors, such as friends and family, or you had to have some method of getting to professional investors like venture capitalists (VCs).

Literally everything about fundraising is easier in the Internet age.

One big time waster for founders used to be pitching investors who weren't a good fit for the company. Now most professional investors post online portfolios showing the kinds of investments they make. You can check their portfolios, read their blogs, and follow them on Twitter.

If you're at an early stage in your planning and need to get to know investors, you can attend local networking events. Check the listings at Meetup.com for networking events near you.

What if you don't know any "angels," investors who'll provide seed capital, management advice, and contacts? An amazing website has emerged called Angel List (www.angel.co). Think of it as a dating site or Craigslist that matches entrepreneurs with investors. Angel List has hundreds of thousands of participants with billions of dollars being invested through the platform. Like a dating site, you need to create a high-quality profile for your company and put your best foot forward. You also need to reach out to investors—you can't wait for them to e-mail you.

Internet-based "crowdfunding" emerged in the late 1990s as an alternative model of financing to support projects, companies, and individuals with ideas. There are hundreds of crowdfunding platforms on the Internet today orchestrating investment for startups.

You'll still want to hire professional legal counsel to manage any documents. The good news is that it's way less expensive and far more standardized than it used to be. Many top VCs and angels use standard legal document forms available online.

However, please take my advice: just because these legal docs are available online doesn't mean you should avoid hiring a lawyer. If you mess up your financing documents, your legal exposure as a founder is significant. Not only are you putting your own equity at risk, but you might run afoul of state and federal securities laws.

These standardized documents, however, have cut seed-stage legal bills from tens of thousands of dollars to single digit thousands. Also, many firms that do early stage company fundraising will defer their fees until after you raise the money if they think your company shows promise.

THE TIME IS NOW

"The best time to plant a tree is twenty years ago. The second best time is now."

– CHINESE PROVERB

Many founders opt to wait until they have sufficient savings and a financial cushion before starting their new business. They anticipate a lower income stream as they build their startup. Savings might come from a previous business event like a bonus, sale of a prior company, or cashing out stock options. In any case, starting a new venture can put considerable strain on a founder's financial resources.

It can be daunting to consider all the fiscal variables when thinking about the right time to start your business. And of course there is always the risk of losing the capital you put into it.

If you haven't yet achieved the financial cushion you feel you need, it doesn't mean you have to delay your founding dreams. Starting a business on the side while you still have your day job allows you to maintain your income while scaling your business.

According to Van Barker, founder of YardStash:

> I chipped away at the YardStash concept when I was working full time. And once it got to the tipping point of being profitable and showing signs of being able to scale, I jumped into being an entrepreneur full time over the last almost twenty four months.
>
> When I quit [my day job], YardStash was profitable. By day five of the month, pretty much I was making a profit. So I could see that if I could ramp volume that there'd be money coming in. I didn't see [a case where] I would have to actually write a check and take a risk on that side. That was my simple math.

Bryan Johnson, founder of the super-successful online payments company Braintree, started his business on the side while he was working at Sears. Johnson had previously worked in sales for a credit card processing company and believed he could provide better service than his old firm.

He approached a number of old customers and was in business. Johnson bootstrapped Braintree until he was doing over $10 million in revenue. Only at that point did he raise venture capital. Braintree is the processor behind Uber, Airbnb, Shopify, and OpenTable, and the company's customers propelled meteoric growth.[14]

There is an inherent danger for prospective founders who delay action until they've achieved a certain level of savings. If your career is progressing well and you are accumulating savings and wealth through bonuses and stock options, you can become dependent on that income stream. You might never budge toward your dream.

Noam Wasserman, professor at Harvard Business School, has studied thousands of founders, young and old. Wasserman believes that older prospective founders can get too used to what he called "golden handcuffs": "Potential late-career founders have to guard against the perils of waiting. They should...maintain a low personal burn rate so they don't get used to the [golden] handcuffs of a high-priced lifestyle...so they can accumulate seed capital for their eventual startup."[15]

The bottom line is that the pull of founding something of your own needs to be stronger than the ties holding you in your current career. The motivations that drive you as a founder—freedom, wealth, control, passion—eventually reach a crescendo. It doesn't have to be a bolt of lightning, but at some point you know you're ready. It's then or never.

Kelly Cooper, founder of men's athletic clothing company QOR, knew it was the right time to leave the large corporate world:

> [On the] corporate side... the short-term benefits are better, the bonus and the incentives. I left a shit load of money, for me, on the table and I didn't look back, because I really wanted to be in an environment where I could be super creative and chart my own destiny, and that's not the way it is in the corporate world.

> At Athleta, some of the designers didn't even know I had a design background because I was so into the weeds in the paperwork... and managing a team, and managing expectations, managing and more managing, as opposed to actually creating or being an entrepreneur or a catalyst for a brand.

> Here [at QOR] that's not the case...We've created something from nothing. It's all kind of new, it's all the unknown, all those things, but...I've always been a risk taker, so it feels right.

Your crescendo can build slowly as you take the time to research your market and competition. That's what Sara Blakely, the founder of Spanx, decided to do. She had never worked in fashion, so she researched all the patents out there and bought all of her competitors' products, learning everything she could about her retail environment.[16]

Starting your business as a side gig can help limit the risk and give some insight into the viability of the new venture. It can also provide some impetus for the time to leap.

YOUR MARKET WINDOW

The time to found your company might be influenced by the market you've decided to pursue. All founders go through a process, some formal and some informal, of evaluating their ideas to see if the market is receptive.

Some ideas have a "market window" which compels the founder to chase the idea now rather than later. There can be a number of factors that go into evaluating your market window. One factor is rapidly changing technology. For example, the explosion of smartphones and "location aware" technologies enabled thousands of mobile app developers to launch companies based on that technology.

Eric Groves, founder and CEO of Alignable, the social network for local business owners, knew when his market window had opened.

> My previous company, Constant Contact, shifted power to local businesses in a way that really hadn't been done for a long time, since QuickBooks came around. The shift basically changed engaging with your customers from a dollar per impression through direct mail to a fraction of a penny through e-mail. And by doing so, it really put the power back in the hands of local businesses to bring their customers back in a really effective way.

Market timing is a tricky proposition, though. If an enabling technology such as GPS on smartphones has yet to emerge, or yet to stabilize around technology standards, then it might make sense to wait to found a company. But trying to nail the "perfect time" could cause you to wait forever, or a little too long.

Another significant factor in evaluating the timing and market opportunity is the competition. Does the market have entrenched competitors? Is your company aiming to radically disrupt the market? If so, you will want to evaluate current competitors' efforts at innovating. A perfect example of this type of startup was Uber. When Uber was launched, the competition was local taxi companies whose service was generally mediocre or poor and who had not employed innovations in serving their customers.

There can be a strong temptation to be "first to market" and it's true that some markets have significant *first mover advantage*. It can be easy, though, to overstate the value of first mover advantage. The first mover often creates or seeds the market and the second or third wave of competitors comes in with a better offering. It is important to remember that Apple did not invent the first digital music player. Facebook did not invent the first social network. Indeed did not invent the first job board.

Just because another company is out there pursuing your idea does not mean you shouldn't pursue it. What's your unique angle? Why will customers choose your offering?

As a mid-life founder, you've had reasons to delay the start of your entrepreneurial journey. Perhaps there is no perfect time to become a founder, but there's never been a better time than now. Keep your eye on that window of opportunity.

WHAT'S YOUR IDEA?

"If opportunity doesn't knock, build a door."

MILTON BERLE, COMEDIAN AND ACTOR

One of the things I hear regularly from people is, "I'd like to start a company but I don't have an idea." Occasionally, a great idea, one worthy of starting a company, hits the founder like a bolt of lightning. More often than not, though, ideas for startups are generated bit-by-bit.

Your idea might come from observation of the world around you. Something that you wish existed in your daily life, a need you can address, or some issue or problem you know you can tackle. Or it might stem from your professional work where you see a "white space" in a market or an industry challenge you can solve.

Your founding idea can be a product or service, an "invention" or innovation that offers a new solution to a pressing need. Solutions are ideal, but many of us aren't quite there yet. We don't have a burning problem to solve—we just know we're itching to start a company. We know we want the freedom of autonomy, a chance to be our own boss, make our own hours, the opportunity to generate wealth outside of a regular paycheck.

There is no single way to come up with an idea, but keep your mind open, observe, read widely, follow business trends, and get in the habit of writing down your emerging ideas. They will grow, shift shape, change, and combine as new ideas surface.

IDEAS FROM YOUR BUSINESS EXPERIENCE

Many of the founders I interviewed for this book were motivated to start their companies by their previous work experience. Eric Groves, for example, had been an early executive at the e-mail marketing company Constant Contact. His new business, Alignable, grew out of his professional experience working with small local businesses to solve their problems:

> Well, I think a lot of it comes out of the experience of being part of a number of early stage businesses that all took different paths... All were very successful in their own right... A lot of the time [I] spent at Constant Contact was...with local businesses and that really opens your eyes, because Constant Contact really was a product that revolutionized the market.
>
> Having spent a lot of time with local businesses, [I really] wanted to do something that significantly improves their ability to

compete and thrive. When you look at it and you think you find an opportunity...where you can really shift the market significantly, then that's what really gets an entrepreneur excited, and that's what got me really excited to go off and do this on my own.

So, when I started thinking about the next piece of the equation, which was, "How do you help local businesses actually acquire new customers?"... [I] came across the notion that local businesses are really operating in isolation, and they're surrounded by such a wealth of knowledge in the form of experiences of other local businesses. Why doesn't a network exist that allows them to interact, on a daily basis, to work on their challenges and their opportunities?

And so, when you see that and you look at that opportunity, you go, "Geez, if we get this right we can really change and tip the competitive marketplace back towards local businesses being much more competitive against the big box retailers and the online retailers and the Amazons of the world through that."

Groves' idea came directly from his industry experience. When you've spent twenty years in an industry, you know your customers; you understand their problems and needs. You have a pretty good sense of the gaps in existing tools and solutions.

When customers complain, consider what needs or concerns are not being met. What are they complaining about? When they defect to a competitor, what are their primary reasons? What products do you wish your company could offer? What do your customers want?

Take them to lunch and find out. Of course be mindful not to compete or solicit business outside your present company. (We'll cover this legal issue more in Chapter 11.) Do they need a product or a service? If you're lucky, you might find startup customers or investors right out of the gate. Finding early customers validates your idea and can produce your first revenue. At the very least, you are expanding and consolidating your network, one of the biggest competitive advantages of a mid-life entrepreneur.

The more you reflect on new ideas, the more open you'll be to trends in your industry and in the business environment at large. Walter Cruttenden, who spent decades in the investment banking and securities industries, saw that the Internet was going to have a huge impact on his ability to reach investors. In the 1990s, he started E-Offering as an investment banking arm of E-Trade. Then as smartphone usage began to grow, he and his son founded Acorns, a new investment company that created a micro-investing mobile app to take advantage of the new mobility of young millennial investors.

> I have four boys, but my son Jeff was the one always interested in the markets. He was just about to graduate as a math major and we were brainstorming. I had seen how costs had been coming down in the industry... We realized that micro-investing was going to be a possibility. Jeff, who was in an investment club at school, realized that all of his buddies wanted to have [investment] accounts. They did not have much more than $50 or $100. They did not want to pay $10 to Schwab because the percentages did not work out too well. We started this micro-investing thing...

The opportunity was to really disrupt the old guys. I think you probably remember when the old firms, Paine Webber, E.F. Hutton, and Smith Barney, and guys like this, they kind of ignored the new online guys that came out when the browser came out. They ignored the Schwab and E-Trade because they did not want to cannibalize their prices. They were hoping it would just be a small business, but of course these things have a way of turning.

You cannot [hold back the tide]... That is kind of what we think is happening now. A broker asking for $5,000 or $10,000 or $50,000 to start an account is unnatural. It is always done for the broker's convenience. It is done for the old economics, enough to get a diversified portfolio. Stuff like that. Today, all these economics have changed. You can start people with fifty cents in the background unannounced. It is just happening.

Kelly Cooper's experience in women's athletic apparel at Athleta led directly to her seeing an opportunity in men's athletic apparel.

I mean, I don't know how many times Athleta customers would say, "We need a version of this for my husband." And, honestly, a significant percentage of our purchasers will be women [buying for their husbands or significant others].

Lululemon, for instance, something like 20 percent of their $1.5 billion business [is for men]. Obviously it's huge for companies like Nike and Under Armour. The market is there and the market hasn't really seen anything like what we're doing...

The investors are the former investors from Athleta. Our CEO developed the concept and pitched it to them and they picked up on it right away and said let's go for it. Again, it was easier because we had a track record. It would be another story if we didn't.

SOLUTIONS TO DAILY PROBLEMS

In contrast to using your work experience as the basis of the startup idea, a large number of founders start their businesses to market solutions to problems they have identified in their daily lives or with their families. These problems might be large or small.

Most of us have used or have heard of travel services Uber and Airbnb. In the case of Uber, founders Travis Kalanick and Garrett Camp were attending the LeWeb conference in Paris when they found they were unable to get a cab. That sparked their idea for UberCab, a solution to the same problem of finding a cab in San Francisco where Camp lived.

Airbnb founders Brian Chesky and Joe Gebbia were struggling to pay their rent in ultra-pricey San Francisco. They turned their loft into lodging space, putting airbeds on the floor and offering guests breakfast. They pushed their idea further at the 2008 Democratic National Convention in Denver to take advantage of the city's shortfall of hotel rooms. Realizing there was a market, they designed a service for people who needed short-term accommodations and for homeowners and apartment renters who needed additional income. They changed the company's original name, Airbed & Breakfast, to

Airbnb after attending the Y Combinator accelerator program.

SOLUTIONS TO YOUR OWN PROBLEMS

Van Barker had been an executive in large corporations before starting YardStash as a solution to storing his kids' bicycles.

> It was one of those ideas where I was looking for a solution. I consider myself a pretty good web searcher...[but] could not find anything to store my children's bikes outside our home, besides an expensive shed. I was able to find one product in England that I ordered...[but] it was really poorly made and disintegrated very quickly. And from there, I interacted with a good friend of mine who's an industrial designer at Hewlett Packard. And we basically said, "We can develop a better mousetrap."

> And from there we just started to prototype the idea, get some feedback. So really, it was born out of finding a product that I thought would be high demand in a pretty good category...something that had potential to be...a product that I could start selling and testing the concept.

For KangaDo founder Sara Schaer, her mobile app company originated from her own challenges transporting her kids to and from school and activities. Similar in ways to Uber, KangaDo coordinates rides among parents and pre-selected, heavily screened drivers.

> Along the way [of my career] I became a mom, and while the advent of smartphones pretty quickly helped me juggle my work life more efficiently, I found that I still had just as much of an

issue trying to plan and find trustworthy help. So I started looking around thinking, *well is there anything here?* This is about 2010 or so when I started asking myself this question, having been through all sorts of permutations of work schedules...running a team across three continents. I didn't find anything looking around at apps that could really help me find the care...[to] trust in and that would fill my [parenting and transportation] needs.

As the kids grew older and the transportation issue became more and more pressing...I felt like, "I can't get this done. I can't be in two places at once. I am often out of town or [away from home]. The kids literally cannot do after-school activities because I am in the office, unless I get help, so long story short that's how the idea for KangaDo was born.

Sara Blakely famously founded her innovative women's hosiery company Spanx after being unable to find pantyhose to meet her needs. Blakely was working in the heat of Florida and did not want pantyhose with feet, so she experimented. When she cut the feet off her pantyhose they rolled up her leg. That wouldn't do. She studied every major product on the market and invested $5,000, her life savings, to produce a prototype. She launched her company from her apartment, doing all the initial sales calls herself. Her big break came when she convinced a Neiman Marcus buyer to carry Spanx in a few stores. Blakely turned her problem and that $5,000 investment into a net worth of over a billion dollars.[17]

Richard Branson is one of the most successful entrepreneurs of our lifetime. His company, Virgin Group, is comprised of more than 400 businesses. Branson once said, "There is no point in starting your own business unless you do it out of a sense of frustration."

He got his start in business selling mail-order records. A few years later, he started a record shop, and then, based on a market opportunity he saw and heard about from artists who couldn't get signed, he started the Virgin Music record label. Virgin Music hit it big by signing artists that few other labels would sign, including The Sex Pistols, Culture Club, and The Human League.[18]

As you encounter challenges in your own life, be aware of them, write them down. Brainstorm solutions. Anytime you find yourself saying "There has to be a better way," make note of it. Think about the way it could become a company.

Be on the lookout for the times when you or someone around you says "I wish that…" about their daily life. Not only the wild dreams like "I wish we could go to Mars," but the day-to-day things like "I wish there were a better way to open a wine bottle."

Keep a notebook or use the notes app on your phone. Try a free app like Evernote on your smartphone and laptop.

HOW TO BRAINSTORM IDEAS

In his book *Choose Yourself*, noted author and entrepreneur James Altucher suggests that we hone and improve our ability to come up with ideas simply by practicing coming up with ideas. Brainstorm ideas in bunches, and you'll gradually develop a sense of which ones are great. The right idea is one you feel passionate about and solves a problem or fills a true market need.

Altucher suggests writing down several ideas every day for a year. Your "idea muscles" need to be exercised so they will become stronger. Try writing down five new ideas a day and see where they lead you.[19]

Starting an inventory of your own skills is another way to begin generating ideas. What is it you do, or what do you know, that people might be willing to pay you for? People have started companies on nothing more than helping kids with math homework. Leveraging your skills can result in a new product, a new app, or a new technology. There are no limits.

My friend Scott Granai started a business with his wife, Beth, around his passion: healthy cooking. Scott loves to cook and did most of the cooking for their family of five. Beth had insisted that the family eat organically and with natural foods. One night, Scott made a barbeque sauce from all natural ingredients. Blown away by it, Beth encouraged Scott to make it again, and they realized they were onto something: a great-tasting, all-natural, organic barbeque sauce. They started Outta The Park Eats (www.outtathepark.com) to bring it to market. Their barbeque sauces are now carried in twenty three states nationwide.

Here are some questions to work through to get your "idea machine" working:

- What frustrates me in the world?
- What do I wish my current company would do for customers?
- If I were a customer of my current company, I would ask for...
- What do I love doing so much that it doesn't feel like work?
- Who really, really needs my skills?
- What could I teach?
- How am I different from all the other people who could teach it?
- What nice things do people say about me?
- What products or services are basically pains in the ass?
- What do I need?
- What company do I dread interacting with?
- What do I know better than anyone else at work?
- If I quit, what would my boss need to replace the most?
- Who has money and what do they need?
- If I had $1,000, what would I buy?
- What companies make me feel good?
- When was the last time that I got more than I paid for?
- What worries me?

If you answer these questions and follow the practice of generating five ideas a day, you'll be well on your way to finding a product or service for your new business.

BIG BANG OR LITTLE BANG?

Dave McClure, founder of the seed fund 500 Startups, believes that startups should focus more on incremental improvements than "big bang" inventions. In a riff on comedian Louis

CK, McClure titled his 2013 PubCon keynote address "Everything Sucks and Nobody Cares."[20] His premise is that products and services that make small improvements are far more likely to succeed in the marketplace than earth-shaking innovations.

Here are some of the small things that McClure thinks suck:

- Grade school
- Dating
- Waiting on hold
- Returning stuff
- TSA/checking in/airport luggage
- Trying to get a waiter's attention
- Public speaking
- Running a startup

McClure's point is that entrepreneurs should "make things suck less" by focusing on incremental improvements over time. If you as a founder can find small improvements that people really crave, you'll have a chance to beat slow-moving incumbents in addressing consumer needs. Make things suck less and you'll have a great company.

You don't have to think like Jeff Bezos, Mark Zuckerberg, or Steve Jobs in order to come up with solutions. Start by making something somewhat better and *keep improving it incrementally*. If you do that, you'll become significantly better than other market alternatives.

HOW TO EVALUATE YOUR IDEA LIKE AN INVESTOR

Before quitting your job, you'll want to test your idea—your business premise or hypothesis. How likely is it to succeed? Even if you don't plan on taking a nickel of outside capital, you should have a sense of the framework investors use to evaluate business ventures. After all, you're an investor, too.

You will be investing your precious time, years of your career, and maybe your savings. The term "sweat equity" refers to all the effort, stress, and even tears invested in new businesses. Evaluating the idea before you start can help you avoid wasting your investment.

My evaluation process comes from years of working with investors who evaluate companies for a living. As an investment banker, I had first-hand experience taking companies public. I observed institutional stock investors in mutual fund companies and pension funds asking questions of management teams. I later put that to use as a venture capitalist myself, investing in early stage companies, often just as they were being formed.

The process of evaluating a business premise involves thinking through some basic questions:

- Does it solve a problem?
- Can you identify a revenue stream?
- How big is the market?
- Can customers use it right now?
- What makes the product or company unique?
- What would it take for it to be big?

Evaluating your ideas really depends on the type of business you plan to build. For example, if you plan to start a new software business, you'll need a team with marketing skills that can also raise venture capital. You'll need a fast-growing market so that you can build a large enough business to produce significant equity value for your investors.

On the other hand, if you are building a lifestyle business, like those described in Tim Ferriss' book *The 4-Hour Workweek*, then market size will not matter nearly as much. What will matter more is that you can sell your product easily over the Internet with fairly limited follow-on support. You will want a product that is easy to ship and one that customers search online, so you can use Google or Amazon as a primary way of locating new customers.

Most first-time entrepreneurs think that investors select certain companies because of the product idea. After all, goes the thinking, a revolutionary product can take over a market because of huge demand. Witness the launch of the iPhone!

However, it doesn't really work that way. In fact, the most important factor for investors is the founding team. Why is that? Early product ideas are often wrong, the market isn't receptive, and the company needs to shift to a new market, developing new products or features.

The team is the constant.

Jo Tango is founder and partner at Kepha Partners, a small but highly successful venture capital fund in Boston. According to Tango:

> I look for people with compelling personal stories as to why they are going to have the mental toughness to persist and succeed. A lot of times when someone is late in their work career and wants to be a founder for the first time, the first question I try to ask is: Why? And the second is: Why now? Why didn't you do this before?

> A lot of founders I know...have grown up in pretty desperate situations and therefore have the need to control their current situation. And [they] are willing to forsake bigger pay, bigger car, bigger title, prestigious company, to do their own thing because they want the control.

Operational and managerial experience can be a huge plus. Many investors will tell you that ideas are of little to no value without *execution*. What they mean by that is the ability to get the new product to market, to listen to customer feedback, to launch and support new products, and to build an effective sales and marketing organization to grow. So having experience in these areas is important.

If you are trying to grow a high-growth company that will raise capital, you will want a founding team that can work together well and has multiple skill sets. As you evaluate your idea, it's important that you think about your team's strengths relative to the idea and the market.

PAIN RELIEF

One of the most important ways to evaluate your idea is by what significant problem it solves for the customer. Customers want pain relief, and they will go out of their way to find it. When they see your product, they'll tune right in. If it works for them, they'll become "evangelists" for your product, your best freelance sales force.

Founder and venture capitalist Josh Linkner takes the analogy one step further in his article "Is your company selling aspirin, or vitamins?"[21] Linkner's premise is that not only does your product need to relieve a pain, it needs to do it quickly. Vitamins can make you healthier and possibly reduce headaches over time but, if you have a really serious headache, you'll drive to an all-night pharmacy at three in the morning for an aspirin.

According to Linkner, "Businesses that service burning demand and visceral human needs tend to accelerate faster and require far less marketing push than those that offer stuff customers can easily live without."

All founders should look for proof that the market wants what their companies are offering. Depending on what stage of development your company is in, the form of proof might vary.

In the earliest stages, one of the easiest ways to check market demand is to check the volume of online searches using Google's keyword research tool (https://adwords.google.com/KeywordPlanner). This will give you detailed insight into the volume of searches on Google for the products you will be selling. You can also search for phrases that describe the problem. Lastly, you can see if search volume for those terms is growing over time, a good indicator of a growth market.

You can also conduct inexpensive customer research using online surveys from vendors like SurveyMonkey. You'll find more on marketing and launching your startup in chapters 8 and 9.

These types of tools are great, but the best way to understand customer need is through direct customer interaction.

Steve Blank is a multiple-time founder and now a guru on startups. In his seminal book, *The Four Steps to the Epiphany*, Blank encourages founders to "get out of the building."[22] He says that inside the walls of the startup there are no facts, only opinions. The way to turn opinions into facts is by testing those opinions with live customers.

This type of face-to-face research is incredibly powerful in setting product direction, and should help convince you and investors that there is a true pain. Customers might reveal subtleties about the problem, or they might reveal that they have much different, and much bigger, problems than the one you've identified. Face-to-face research also informs you about the solution to the pain. Customers might have built internal solutions or tried other vendors' products and found them lacking. Listen to them.

MARKET RESEARCH

You should evaluate the market that you are trying to penetrate along a number of dimensions.

Venture capitalists and other investors will care a lot more about the size and dynamics of your market because they are trying to build billion-dollar businesses. If your aims are smaller, then the evaluation of the market is less critical, but it is still important for you.

In any case, an understanding of your market is important because it will help you identify and reach your customers with products and services that meet their needs. Ask yourself a few questions:

How large is this market?

Larger markets often have room for more companies and enable you to build a larger company to serve them.

Is it local, regional, national, or global?

This will have an impact on how you find your customers and how you service them.

How fast is it growing?

Fast-growing markets often produce more opportunity for innovators because buyers are regularly evaluating new offerings.

An example of a fast-growing market is craft beers. In 2014, the craft beer market saw a 22 percent rise in retail dollar sales. Drinkers of craft beer are likely to try new beers rather than sticking with Budweiser or even their favorite microbrew.

Are the incumbents (existing companies) slow-moving and ripe for disruption or are they fast and innovative?

Increasingly, we are seeing new businesses take on incumbents and grow at phenomenally fast rates. A company like Uber is a perfect example. The market for local transportation, particularly for taxis and limos, had not adopted new technologies, and its users were very dissatisfied. Uber came along offering a better way. Punch a button on your smartphone and a ride comes to pick you up. Payment is handled automatically through your credit card. Uber was founded in 2009 and, according to *Business Insider*, produced over $10 billion in gross revenue in 2014. That's a market that was ripe for disruption.

How do customers prefer to buy? Do they repeat their purchases?

Understanding how your customers buy is incredibly important to building your sales channels and your product. If you're selling to businesses (B2B), do they buy direct or through distributors, or perhaps both? An example of both would be a software company that sells directly to customers, but also offers its product through system integrators or consultants who can help manage the installation and customization. The fast-growing customer relationship management product Salesforce works like this.

Do customers prefer to try the product before they use it?

Most software products offer some kind of trial. Usually the vendor offers either a free trial period, or they offer a free version that has a limited set of features, with the enticement to purchase the full product.

Are there enabling technologies or other elements that need to be in place before your market takes off?

Most people probably don't remember the Apple Newton, the first mobile interactive device. It was a huge flop. It's not that the idea was a bad one—it was just too far ahead of its time. Fast forward twenty five years, and Apple sells 50 million iPads every year.

The rapid adoption of smartphones was an enabling technology for apps, games, photo manipulation and sharing (like Instagram), and mobile payments (like Square). Small, free utilities like apps and PC games existed before smartphones, but the user experience, the distribution model, and the *need* all changed radically.

MARGIN

One of the important elements in evaluating your product idea is "margin." If you're not familiar with accounting, margin is the amount of money you have at the end of the day after all the costs of doing business. And the most important margin calculation is "gross margin."

Gross margin accounts for the cost of the product itself, not all the other costs of running the business. For example, if you're selling a retail product, its gross margin is revenue minus the costs of making or procuring the product. If you sell pens for $1 and it costs you 80 cents to purchase, then your gross profit is twenty cents and your gross margin is 20 percent.

The reason gross margin is so important is that high gross-margin products, like information products or software, can produce significant bottom-line profits at the end of the day. They enable the company to invest significant amounts in sales and marketing. These types of businesses can generate cash for growth.

YOUR BUSINESS MODEL

The term "business model" is somewhat overused by investors. It refers to the way a company is set up to make money. "Business model" refers to the revenue sources, sales and marketing channels, products, and ultimately the path to profitability.

Here are a few examples:

- A print or online media company makes money through advertising. They bring consumers to the website and run various forms of advertising. Advertisers pay for the right to run ads in front of those consumers.
- Google also makes money through advertising, but Google uses what is called "performance advertising." Do you see

all those links at the top of the Google search results and on the right hand side? Google gets paid only when a consumer clicks on one of those. This is called "pay-per-click."

- Most B2B software companies use a direct sales model. This can be either a "field" sales team that meets with large customers or an "inside" team that calls and e-mails customers.

- Consumer product companies can sell directly through a website (e-commerce) or through large retailers like Amazon or Walmart. Hundreds of large and small companies have launched and grown by selling directly via e-commerce, such as Zappos, Wayfair, Bonobos, 1800Contacts, and Dollar Shave Club.

- Mobile app vendors, and many software companies, use what is called a "freemium" model, a mashup of the words "free" and "premium." In this model, the basic product is free for consumers to use, but enhanced features cost money. The premium versions are advertised regularly inside the free product and through e-mail. A small percentage of the overall user base will upgrade and pay, but the company depends on this group to be large enough to cover its costs. Good examples of freemium products are Evernote, LinkedIn, and most mobile games.

In the early days, you might not yet know your exact business model. You should have a hypothesis, though, and I will walk you through a simple but structured approach for creating one in Chapter 8.

CONSIDER THE COMPETITION

Understanding your competition is important in a new business. In some rare cases, competition can kill a new company. Are your competitors mostly small companies who are all trying to "create" a market? Or are they larger, slower-moving companies from whom you can take share by having a better product or better service?

One thing that many entrepreneurs worry about is that some competitor will "steal" their idea. This rarely happens. Far more new businesses die from lack of interest than from competition.

Healthy competition can be a good thing for a new business. Competition can help focus a business by putting a target on something. It can help in goal setting and in articulating the value proposition of your business. See the marketing section on "positioning" in Chapter 9.

There are some real benefits to competition. Competition validates your concept. As much as you might worry about besting another company, it sure beats trying to create a market or convince a customer that they have a problem in the first place.

You can draft behind competitors. They create an anchor point in customers' minds about pricing and features that you can beat. You don't have to be better than the competition in all cases, only for your specific customer segment.

Facebook was not the first social network. MySpace and

Friendster were the first to achieve customer success. Apple was not the first portable MP3 player. There were dozens of others, but Apple created a much easier to use interface and a better way to acquire music (through the iTunes store), so the iPod flourished. Don't be scared off by competition. Know how you're going to be better and how you're going to execute.

CAN YOUR BUSINESS SCALE?

Can your business grow profitably and acquire lots of customers quickly? Can you manage that growth? Can your business adapt to increased demand? This is what investors mean by "scalability."

There are many components to scalability. Some of these relate to your product. If it's a physical product, will you be able to get enough units at high quality? If it's an information or tech product, can you handle lots of customers?

Many of the questions about scale are operational ones. At the early evaluation phase, you don't need to know the answers to scaling questions, but it is helpful to have thought through what the challenges may be.

In fact, at the early phases when you're first proving your idea, it can be helpful to do things that won't scale. This sounds counterintuitive. However, in the early phase, the important thing is proof that customers like your idea, not that it can scale. You can put processes and technology in place to help scale later.

As founder of the business incubator Y Combinator, Paul Graham has invested in and helped mentor dozens of successful startups, including Airbnb, Dropbox, Reddit, and Stripe. Graham wrote a blog post for founders called "Do Things That Don't Scale."[23] He emphasizes that startups often have to recruit new users manually and walk them through a trial of the idea. The early days for Airbnb consisted of going door to door to recruit hosts who might rent out a room.

> Airbnb now seems like an unstoppable juggernaut, but early on it was so fragile that about thirty days of going out and engaging in person with users made the difference between success and failure.

> You'll be doing different things when you're acquiring users a thousand at a time, and growth has to slow down eventually. But, if the market exists, you can usually start by recruiting users manually and then gradually switch to less manual methods.

> You should take extraordinary measures not just to acquire users, but also to make them happy. For as long as they could, which turned out to be surprisingly long, Wufoo sent each new user a hand-written thank you note. Your first users should feel that signing up with you was one of the best choices they ever made. And you in turn should be wracking your brain to think of new ways to delight them.

IS IT SUSTAINABLE?

Most businesses that get past the early stage and grow and sustain their operations have an advantage in the market.

Depending on how large a business you want to build and how quickly you plan to grow it, you will seek out different types of sustainable advantage:

- Location
- Technology
- Know-how
- Service
- Customer intimacy
- Network effects

Every investor will want to know if you can sustain that competitive advantage. Is there intellectual property you can patent? Is there a network effect that can drive your growth, as with companies like LinkedIn or Instagram? Will you be able to keep your customers coming back because of incredible service, like Zappos, or because they love the experience of your products, like Apple or Dropbox?

Sustainability is one of many factors we've explored in this chapter to take into consideration when generating ideas for your new business. You've also learned a number of ways to assess your ideas. These principles and methods are key for mid-life entrepreneurs since they help you manage your risk by finding the ideas with the best chances of success.

HIRING YOUR TEAM &
BUILDING YOUR CULTURE

---

*"The secret of change is to focus all
of your energy not on fighting the
old, but on building the new."*

SOCRATES

So much is made of building a *great* team for your startup, and rightly so, but you don't hear nearly as much about building the *right* team. By "right team," I mean a team that fits your personality, skills, and values.

A team that will work hard, persevere through tough times, and go the extra mile to take care of customers is often the difference between startup success and failure. So it's important to think about what kind of team and culture you want for your company.

Culture is a funny thing in a startup. There are people who will tell you that culture starts from the top, that leaders set the tone. Others believe that it comes from the bottom, from the rank-and-file employees who build the product, interface with customers, and deliver service. I actually think both are true. Culture is an articulation of values and norms and how you live them.

David Mandell spent the first half of his career in corporate roles and consulting with Deloitte before joining a series of smaller companies. He is now founder and CEO of PivotDesk, an office space marketplace. Mandell spoke bluntly about culture: "A lot of people think culture is based on foosball tables and catered lunches...but that's all bullshit. What you need is an organization that enjoys working together, because that's when they work best."

There are good reasons to start thinking about culture *now*, before you've incorporated your business or even started looking for cofounders. Culture is at the core of what you'll be looking for both in cofounders and your first hires.

In a company with only a few people, relationships can work really well or not at all. Your small team is going to get your product or service out the door, keep your customers happy, and set the stage for future growth. So your culture is vital.

CULTURE BASICS

Until now, you've been part of company cultures that already existed. Now you'll be establishing a company culture based on the values you choose. So let's look at a few questions to help elicit clarity and focus:

What traits do you really value in colleagues?

Who have been the best people you've worked with in your career? Why? What made them so good in your eyes?

Who do you respect the most as a boss? Why? Who do you respect least? Why?

What kinds of things are you good at and want to do more of?

What energizes you professionally?

What things de-energize you?

One of the great things about starting a company at this point in your career is you probably know yourself pretty well. You've learned patience and perseverance. Your personality is fairly developed and stable. You know what works and what doesn't in a career setting. You've hungered for a creative work environment in which people can innovate and contribute to their greatest potential. This is your opportunity to build a workplace culture.

As one of the cofounders of the Techstars incubator program, Brad Feld has worked with dozens of successful startups at his firm Foundry Group. In regard to company culture, Feld believes there are some real differences between older and younger entrepreneurs:

Older entrepreneurs tend to be in a narrower band around personality in forming a team. In other words, they are a little clearer about what their personality is and how they want to build a team...around them.

Younger entrepreneurs can be more chaotic. They are less developed in their personality and their behaviors. When their personality comes out, it can be in more surprising and unexpected...ways. There is a wider range.

Older entrepreneurs are more constrained by family, friends, and their life situation, so there is less variability. This has a lot to do with building a culture.

In younger entrepreneurs, their point of view on culture and what they want is evolving. With older entrepreneurs, their point of view is more stable.

CO-FOUND OR FLY SOLO?

One of the first decisions you'll have to make is whether to start the company yourself or work with cofounders. This decision is deeply personal and impacts the kind of company you build.

Starting a flower shop is not the same as building a software startup or biotech company. There are different technical hurdles, different capital requirements, different marketing and sales features, and different exit paths.

Your decision to work with cofounders or fly solo will be

impacted not only by the type of business, but by who you are and what you love to do. Some entrepreneurs will go it alone until they have some traction, then seek cofounders.

One of the best reasons to work with a cofounder is to add to the skills of the team. Compatibility is important, but not by itself. We don't just partner with or hire people because they are friends. You need to add critical skills in marketing, product development, finance, sales, and design.

Cofounders are great sounding boards for handling challenging decisions. Rather than having to work through problems on your own, a cofounder can help you think things through. They can help you see alternate approaches and run scenarios.

Angel investor Reid Hoffman, cofounder of LinkedIn, suggests that media have made startup founders out to be supermen and superwomen. He spoke to this concern in a lecture at Stanford University in 2014:

> One way, I think, to explode the myth of super-founder is [that] usually it's best to have two or three people on a team rather than a solo founder. It's not to say that solo founders don't actually play out...successfully, but most often two or three people is much better.
>
> I look at these things as an investor, and...[ask], "What is a good composition of a project and founders that are likely to succeed?" It's usually two or three of them. What great founders do is seek the networks that will be essential to their task."[24]

Cofounders contribute to the culture of the business and help you reinforce those values when you hire staff. It is much easier to share accountability than to have it all on your own shoulders. A cofounder is there with you when things go off track. It's like training for a marathon together, or having a support team when you're trying to lose a few pounds. Someone is in it with you, and that provides emotional lift.

When I began my first startup, I didn't really think this through deeply enough. Going it alone turned out to be more difficult and lonely than I had expected.

Facebook founder Mark Zuckerberg commented on this subject in a 2014 town hall meeting:

> No person knows how to deal with everything. But if you can find a team of people, or friends, or family—and there will be different people over time, because different people like to focus on different problems or different scales of...problems—then that's what's really going to get you through.
>
> That's what's gotten me through and that's what continues to get me through all the stuff that we have. Yeah, you don't have to be superhuman, you have to just kind of keep on going and not do it alone, and find people who share your passion for what is the important thing in the world."[25]

There is a ton of work in any early stage company, and having a cofounder means the work will be shared. However, there also are good reasons to be a solo entrepreneur, regardless of the type of business you are starting.

Most importantly, there is no one with whom to disagree. Founder disagreements are one of the largest causes of startup failure. When founders break up, it does significant damage to the company, so much so that often the company dies.

Noam Wasserman of Harvard Business School studied the subject extensively for his book, *The Founder's Dilemmas*. Wasserman found that 65 percent of high-potential startup companies failed as a result of conflict among the cofounders.[26]

Another reason to stay solo is that it's sometimes more productive to just do it yourself.

Lew Cirne has built two very successful software companies, Wily Technology and New Relic, valued at $400 million and more than $1.5 billion, respectively. Cirne started both companies with no cofounders. While he later hired great employees and management teams, in the beginning Cirne felt he'd be more productive creating the product by himself:

Some creative efforts, just like music, can only be created by a collaboration of a small number of people, while other people are just solo singer/songwriters. I use this analogy all the time. I think of myself as a singer/songwriter in software because I conceive of the product, but then...I actually do the work to build it, too. I think of my business and my product as heavily intertwined early on.

If you decide to work with a cofounder, what should you look for? In what ways should you be the same? In what ways should you be different? Have you worked together before?

Can you give it a trial run?

You don't have to like each other, but you do have to respect each other. There will be make-or-break decisions that will come up. Sometimes you'll disagree.

One way to go about deciding is to use the old interview measure called "the airport test." Basically, you ask yourself, "Would I want to be stuck in an airport with this person?" As a measure of partnership with a founder, it can be quite a useful test. You aren't just considering social compatibility, but a sense of mutual respect and collaborative decision making.

If you're not sure, the important thing is to keep an open mind and start moving the company forward. It might become clearer as you progress and start to hit obstacles.

Mark Suster, a two-time founder turned venture capitalist, thinks it's more important to get started on one's own before trying to find a perfect cofounder.

> Even if you *think* you know them, people change. I say, go ahead and take the leap if you want to start a company... Hire your cofounder [later]. Give them a large sum of equity—20, 30, even 40 percent vested over four years. If you ever fall out of love, you have a pre-nuptial agreement... Truly treat them like a cofounder. Give them access to all confidential information. Involve them in fundraising, hiring, strategy... Publicly call them a cofounder.[27]

Finding a cofounder, whether you do it before you start or after as Suster suggests, is as much an art as a science. You need someone who shares your vision, someone with whom you're compatible, and who wants the same outcome as you do. Maybe you don't want a big venture capital-backed company, just a small, sustainable, profitable business.

You and your cofounder should have differences as well.

Startup expert and early Apple marketing head Guy Kawasaki suggests that cofounders should differ in expertise, orientation, and perspective.

> Founders need to complement each other to build a great organization. Some people like to sweat the details (microscopes). Others like to ignore the details and worry about the big issues (telescopes). The more perspectives, the merrier. These can include young versus old, rich versus poor, male versus female, urban versus country, engineering versus sales, techie versus touchy, Muslim versus Christian, straight versus gay, Android versus iOS, and Macintosh versus Windows.[28]

SELF-ASSESSMENT EXERCISE

Your company's culture is an articulation of you and the type of company you want to build. However, a company culture evolves, just as people do. The evolution of your company culture is shaped by three things:

1. The people you hire
2. The policies you put in place, formally or informally
3. The behavior of the boss and other executives

Take out a sheet of paper. On the left hand side, write down all the professional skills you're really good at. Think about big categories, like selling, recruiting, finance, marketing, customer support. Then try to get a little more detailed. You might not be a "finance" person, but you might be really good at creating a spreadsheet model of something. You might not be in sales, but you might be really good at networking. Focus more on the skills than on the function.

On the right hand side of the paper, write down all the things you aren't good at, or really don't like to do. Try to get pretty detailed. For me, I'm pretty good at the planning part of finance, like modeling our startup's financial plan, but I don't like bookkeeping tasks at all. I find them hugely draining.

In the right hand column will be some skills that are crucial to your startup's success. These are skills you'll need to have in place during the first twelve months. Circle these crucial skills on your list. These are things you're not good at, so you'll need to learn to do them or hire them out to an employee or contractor, or find a friend/volunteer/intern who will take them on.

Notice, you're beginning to create a hiring plan for your startup.

Now we're going to move to values. Start a list of ten to twenty values you think are important. What are the values that really matter to you in building your company and culture?

If you struggle with this, think back to the people you have loved working with. What did you love about them? Was it how they got stuff done? Were they optimistic? Did they always show respect? Did they truly value the customer? Did you like their candor? Their action orientation? Were they fearless or measured in risk taking? Were they resourceful?

An important part of this exercise is to realize that there can be tradeoffs, especially when values are put into practice. For example, someone who is intensely focused on serving the customer might not be as focused on profit or frugality. Someone who is a very honest communicator might sometimes not be regarded as a team player because they can ruffle some feathers.

You'll probably need to come back to this exercise a few times. My recommendation is to narrow your list down to four to six core values to emphasize in hiring and running your company. It's not that other things aren't as important, but you need several essential core values to establish a company culture.

As a founder, you want a culture geared for success in particular, values that are customer-centric and model mutual respect for colleagues, adaptability, and work/life balance. Most of all, your company culture should reflect *you*.

The value suggestions that follow are by no means complete, only possibilities to get you started:

Passionate	Improvement-oriented	Energetic
Customer-focused	Collaborative	Learning-oriented
Innovative	Risk-tolerant	Open
Diverse	Rules-oriented	Warm
Growth-oriented	Process-based	Family-oriented
Competitive	Relentless	Entrepreneurial
Respectful	Quality-oriented	Safe
Ownership-oriented	Timely	Reliable
Service-oriented	Frugal	Fearless
Curious	Adaptable	Data-driven

BUILDING A TEAM THAT FITS

Once you have your list, you'll want to think about how to hire for those qualities. What types of questions will you ask? You could use team interviews or a series of solo interviews. Your reference checks can ask for anecdotes that support these values.

Adding new members to the team will impact your culture, so it's important to hire to the culture you want. In a larger company this is far less important, but in a small startup it's critical. Team members will interact with each other and customers. They might be part of future hiring.

Art Papas, founder of the highly successful software company Bullhorn, Inc., implemented a system to screen for culture during the interview process. He applies this system to reinforce the culture during the company's annual reviews and bonus compensation process. (I used to work at Bullhorn and reported to him.) Although he's not a mid-life entrepreneur, his approach to culture and hiring is one of the most effective I have ever seen.

Papas defines his company's core values in five key phrases or behaviors:

- Ownership
- Energy
- Agility and speed
- Service
- Being human

He and his team go further than just listing values. Along with his company's HR head and executive team, he defines what those phrases mean in terms of behavior. They use everyday examples so that employees and prospective employees know what matters and whether or not they're a good fit. For example, the team defines the value "Energy" in behavioral terms:

- Build up your teammates.
- Leave people positively charged.
- If you see a problem, present constructive feedback directly to the source.
- Act in the interest of the team.
- Accept critical feedback with an open mind.
- Make people want to work with you again.

Equally important, Papas' core values include definitions of *what not to do*. For Energy, they are:

- Talk behind people's backs.
- Stir the pot.

Noting positive and negative examples of behavior can be extremely valuable both in hiring and reviewing. It helps to explain and drive home the values you want to cultivate. It shows newer employees how to hire and what to look for when interviewing. It shows the company how to behave and how not to behave. It enables managers to nip bad behavior in the bud by explaining what the employee did that was not in line with your core values. And importantly, it helps shine a light on employees who are poor cultural fits so that their behaviors can be corrected, or they can be removed from the company.

It might sound harsh, but removing poor fits is just as important in a small business as removing poor performers. The poor fit will bring down the performance of the whole team. The old saying "Hire slowly, fire fast" was never more true than in a small company.

David Mandell of PivotDesk has a perfect example of this situation in the early days of a company:

> I have such experience with bad examples over the course of my career and I've seen so many different people do the wrong thing. But that frame of reference makes making decisions much easier. And if you're a younger entrepreneur, you test that more often because you don't have the experience base. And it can come back to haunt you.

We had an example early on in PivotDesk history where we were working with a developer who was an amazingly talented developer. Young guy. And he started out [as a] contractor and we were discussing him coming on full time because he was doing amazing work. And he said, "Look, I'm happy to come on full time, but here's what I need: I need a CTO title, I need this, and this is how it's got to work." And my cofounder, who didn't have quite the experience [I did], he said, "Well, this guy is quite good, we should think about this," and I said, "No, get rid of him." Because I knew immediately—I had seen that personality before, and I had seen how, regardless of skill set, how that personality can destroy a company.

There is a reason people say "Culture eats strategy for breakfast." Many, many startups go through a dilemma like this one. What do you do about the star employee who is extremely good at his job but who simply does not get along and breaks a lot of glass? Do you fire him? Leave him in place? Reward her with a bonus because she's really good?

This is where your culture and leadership are really tested. There isn't a right answer, but rest assured that everyone will pay attention to the way you handle it, and will act accordingly.

If culture is more important than performance, you will discipline the employee or even fire him. If performance is really the thing that matters, then you'll give him a bonus. But all of your other employees will know, because many of them don't get along with this star. And if you reward the star, it will be hard for you or other leaders to say that getting along or respecting your colleagues is really the thing you value the most.

You also need to think about how your own behavior impacts the culture. Everyone sees what the boss does, from the hours you keep to the way you speak with employees and colleagues to the way you dress. Your employees will emulate you in large part because they want to get ahead.

One of the great things about having a few decades of experience is that you should have a really good sense of who you are. You know what you stand for. You know what inspires you and what pisses you off. You also know what you love to do professionally and what drains you.

So in building your team, not just your founding team but your first ten to fifteen hires, you have an opportunity to find people who fit with you. At this point in your career, you likely have a network to use in recruiting your cofounders and early employees. There is no better proof of how you will work with someone than having worked with them before. Your network can also provide first-hand references—casting a wider net on potential hires.

Don't be afraid to do a little inventory of the qualities you're looking for in hires. I don't simply mean skills, but values, family, personality, and style. Think about, articulate, and write down those qualities you're trying to build in your startup.

When Lew Cirne started his second company, New Relic, he was in a different stage of life than with his earlier company. He thoughtfully built New Relic's culture to reflect these changes:

When I started the company before I had a Series A [funding], the kind of ground rules I had was we're going to look for a more experienced employee base, capable of doing more in a shorter period of time, and is less likely to burn out. We're going to have a standard minimum three-week vacation policy. We're going to encourage people to take all of it and not store it up. You know the rationale, a two-week vacation policy is crazy in my mind. You need three weeks of vacation every year, because I think you ought to be trying to string two weeks together where you are really disconnecting so that you can really recharge.

The other thing I thoughtfully put into the culture is I make a habit of leaving the office at 5:00 every night because one of the important things to me is dinner with the family, and I like to cook the dinner...it is just a routine I have. Certainly I want it not to be, "Oh, Lew the founder gets away with it," but it's a pretty quiet office between 5:00 and 5:30 at New Relic, compared to most other high-growth companies.

I want New Relic employees to love their Mondays. I use that term all the time. I ask people, "Do you love your Mondays?" And I happen to love my Mondays. I think it's an important way to think about it. [There are] two fundamental reasons why I love my Mondays and [why] I want New Relic employees to love their Mondays. One is you love the work you do, you feel like it matters, and it has impact and it gives you joy. And [two is] you love the people you work with. They bring out the best in you and they encourage you and they help you grow.

What are the must haves in your new hires? For many entrepreneurs it's adaptability or resilience, because the entrepreneur understands that the employee's role is likely going to change significantly. Also, there will be meaningful setbacks. How does the prospective employee deal with change? How do they handle getting knocked down?

PivotDesk founder David Mandell puts it this way:

> I think the single most important attribute that I look for in employees...is respect...for everyone in the organization... I mean that at every level of the organization. So...being a senior person does not in any way give you the right to be disrespectful to a junior person. Everyone...is here because they are really good at what they do. Some may have a lot more experience than others, but they're all really good people, and they are all critical to our success. And the second anyone in our organization shows lack of respect, I virtually stop everything and we either fix it or we make a change.

> One of the things we do when we interview people is to get them to interview with employees at every level. To a certain degree, it's the people at the junior level [whose] input...is almost most important to me. Because I want to know how they [the candidate] interacted with them. Did they act like, *Oh, it's a junior person so I don't care?* Or were they truly interested in what that person was doing and their skills?

> The other thing we do, when we ask about prior history and prior experience, we ask for stories and challenges... You can tell based on how they talk about their past history whether they're team people or individual people.

It's also crucial to know yourself and the things you like to do and want to do. Lew Cirne of New Relic knew he didn't want to be "sitting in meetings" or "dealing with extensive pipeline reviews," so he hired brilliant people to do those things.

Here's where you have an advantage over a younger entrepreneur. As Cirne suggests, your personality and skills are pretty well-developed at this point in your career. You have the self-awareness to hire compatible personality types with complementary skills.

> This is a major thing for a founder starting their company later [in life]. The difference between me running Wily (author's note: in his twenties) and me running New Relic (author's note: in his forties) comes back to that self-awareness and self-discovery. I'm far more comfortable with me as I am, with weakness and warts and all, instead of trying to be...someone I wasn't. I don't get excited about crawling through pipeline reviews and looking at [sales] deals and making sure we have a disciplined process for scaling the organization. And I don't like to sit in meetings.

> All of these things are super important for growing and leading a company, but I discovered what I love to do is create stuff. I love to kind of convince other people to join the cause. I love getting people excited about the cause. I've got a list of things I love to do. But then I need to hire for the other things that most people think of as CEO responsibilities. I need to hire very senior people that might otherwise be CEOs and give big responsibilities [to] them.

> So the result, for me personally, is I'm sitting around a table that

has six chairs, and this is the only place where I have meetings. If the meeting has more than six people, unless it's a board meeting, I don't need to be in it. I think it's very rare that someone in their twenties has that much self-awareness to really know... [how] to hire to complement their weaknesses.

And be comfortable letting go. Because as a founder, you have to be passionate about the company and you've got to care about the details, but yet you've got to be comfortable letting go of those details, so that other people can really grow and blossom.

For Kelly Cooper, her challenge was trying to balance cultural fit with the creative brilliance and raw talent needed in designing apparel:

Philosophically, my partners and I had this debate early on [and it's ongoing]. I always say it's 51 percent talent and 49 percent personality. For design, I do need the talent to be there. That to me is ever so slightly more important than soft skills. For me, I need to have that 1 percent more on the talent side. [I still look for] 49 percent personality, meaning they have to be a cultural fit for the brand and respectful of the other people on the team. We don't discount it; it is definitely not 90/10. I just lean 1 percent more on the talent side. But again, at the end of the day, yes, personality is really important to us. We are in close quarters—literally 1,000 square feet.

As for the challenges of having to pass on talent because of personality issues, Cooper had this to say:

On the flip side, personality issues sometimes just can't be managed away. That's why the balance [between talent and personality] is so delicate and important. Managing personality issues can usurp any benefits on the talent side. The fewer the distractions, the more creative and effective the team can be. At the end of the day, everyone's focus needs to be on the product and the customer and, ultimately, the brand.

Brad Handler, the founder of Exclusive Resorts and Inspirato, knew that with his first hires he was looking for people to challenge the status quo. He started out working with recruiters, but he and his cofounder (his brother) were rejecting all of the recruiters' candidates, even though they had impressive track records and significant experience. One recruiter asked, "Why are you rejecting these candidates? They are my best soldiers." Handler responded, "We're not looking for soldiers; we're looking for Green Berets."

YOUR HIRING PROCESS

It's critical to know what you need in new hires. How innovative, how resilient, how exceptional a team do you need? Handler wanted outstanding people, and that's okay, because he knew what he needed.

Handler continued:

> The key is to hire people who know more than you, are smarter than you, are better than you. Otherwise you're never going to learn. That realization allows you to hire Green Berets. A lot of folks I see in startups think they're the smartest guy in the room, and that they can do all of it. We have been successful

because we rightly admit that we can't do any of it without the right people around us.

At this point in your career, you might have already hired and perhaps fired a fair number of people. But hiring in a startup is different than hiring in a big or mid-size company. Startup teams are smaller and therefore the stakes for each individual hire are larger. Most founders involve the whole team or a large portion of it to make sure the fit is right.

Jack O'Toole and Joe BelBruno, founders of CleanAir Sensor Corp., took a "try before you buy" approach to finding great people.

> We interviewed...and then brought [our engineers] on as interns last summer. We got to spend six months working with those engineers, and to me that's a good long time to evaluate whether someone is going to be a contributor or not.

> Our engineers have all either done projects for us or interned for us before we hired them. And then we hired them.

John Levisay, founder of Craftsy, knew what his priorities were for new hires:

> I [look for people who are] intrinsically motivated, and people who would take it personally if it failed. People who really were in it with both feet. It wasn't an ephemeral, "Yeah, I'll give it a try," [but] more like, "We're going to make this work come hell or high water." While we may not socialize a ton, you're spending sixty to seventy hours a week together, [so] you've got to like them.

Or at least have similar ethical and life views that...you're aligned on. You're going to spend two-thirds of your waking hours with these people. You get to a certain age...after forty [where you think] *I'm too old to work with assholes.*

New hires know there's an element of risk in working for a startup. You therefore have to impart a sense of excitement in the mission of your company. The first place to do that is in your job descriptions.

Most job descriptions are boring as hell and written in company or industry jargon. They're all about requirements. You need to change that up. Make it about the prospective candidate. Turn the job description into 50 percent marketing document, 50 percent job description.

Why should they want to work for your company? Why should they even be interested? You're taking on the world? Tell them. You're an amazing manager and you will provide room for growth? Tell them. You offer equity in the business and a chance to learn a ton? Tell them that, too.

If you're not sure how to write a job description, go to Indeed, Venture Beat, and Angel List and read a few. You'll see how many of them suck, and you'll see a few that inspire you. If you were the candidate, what would attract you to the job?

After you get a candidate interested, you need to sell. Startups don't have an established brand. Prospects need to hear your pitch about why you started the company. They need to be sold. Even if the hire is going to report to someone else, you are the person who took the leap, who started the business, and you are the one best able to convince others to come with you on this journey. They need to hear your passion. In fact, they *want* to hear it.

USE YOUR NETWORK AND "SOURCE" CONTINUALLY

With a few decades of work experience behind you, you've amassed contacts, friends, and colleagues—in short, your network. Your network is perhaps the most valuable tool you have when it comes to hiring. Your network can provide candidates, direct referrals, indirect referrals, and reference checks. If you use your network effectively, you can find great people with amazing skills, wonderful attitudes, and shared values.

Keep your network contacts fresh using tools like LinkedIn or Google Contacts (part of Gmail). If you're not using one of those tools, be sure to use a contact management or CRM system to "tag" functionality so that you can organize and reorganize your contacts.

Organize your network into a few simple bucket groups. One group will be "people I want to hire." You'll probably want to segment this further into functions like sales, marketing, finance, and product development. Another bucket is "people who may know others I'd want to hire."

One of the CEO's primary jobs is to find and hire "A" players for all roles. This is an ongoing process. You need to be sourcing top talent continuously, not only when you have job openings.

I'm not suggesting that you interview people for jobs that don't exist. It is important, however, to get to know top talent and to keep in regular touch with them, checking in every few months with a quick e-mail or phone call.

People will really appreciate your efforts and will be much more willing to listen when you are looking. In this way, you'll have a steady flow of inbound candidates. You never know when one of your key employees might get poached by another company, so it's always a good idea to have people in your network who could step in.

Be the keeper of the culture. You've spent time creating it and articulating it, so you want to be sure your hires are a good fit. You need people who'll grow with it, because culture is a living thing, not just words on a page.

LAUNCHING YOUR
NEW BUSINESS

---

*"Everybody has a plan until they
get punched in the mouth."*

MIKE TYSON, FORMER WORLD HEAVYWEIGHT CHAMPION

Part of the reason new businesses have such a high failure rate is that so many entrepreneurs fail to outline their assumptions about how their business will operate; in short, once you have a business idea to pursue, you need to create a business plan.

This might sound intimating, but I don't mean a big long document that spells out everything. That's old school. In today's startup world, business plans are obsolete only moments after you write them. Extensive market research and detailed financial plans will be wrong as soon as you change any element of the business, such as the price point, the marketing channel, or certain features. So what I'm talking about here is a brief, one-page description of "assumptions."

A MODEL ONE-PAGE PLAN

There are a number of templates out there to help you write a one-page plan. My favorite is Lean Canvas, created by Ash Maurya (http://practicetrumpstheory.com/why-lean-canvas). It takes its name from the "Lean Startup" movement that emphasizes moving quickly and staying small until you have validated many of your assumptions.[29]

Start by thinking through and writing down your most important assumptions about your startup. You likely have a bunch of thoughts swimming in your head. Most people tend to start with the product or service first. I suggest trying to put some structure to your thinking and writing down your assumptions. For starters, consider these questions:

- What problem does your product solve?
- What is your product or service?
- Who are your target customers?
- What is really unique about your product/service?
- How are you planning to distribute your product to customers?
- Where will your revenue come from?
- What are your major costs?

If you're doing online research or reading founders' blogs or Reddit, you'll find this process referred to as "finding product/market fit." It's a key step in bringing any new concept to market. While it was originally conceived for innovative technology or mobile products, it has huge value in bringing *anything* to market, including services and blogs. It focuses attention on your customer and your company's point of differentiation (what your business does differently and better).

Lean Canvas isolates nine areas related to "Market" and "Product" in its one-page business model, as shown in the accompanying graphic. It diagrams your one-page structure.

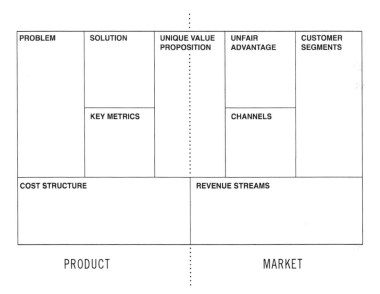

Lean Canvas is licensed under the Creative Commons Attribution-Share Alike 3.0 Un-ported License, via LeanStack.com.

1. PROBLEM

We start on the Product side of the canvas. Write down the top three problems your potential customers have that you intend to solve. It might just be one problem or need. Remember, if there's no problem that needs to be solved, there's no reason to turn to your company for a product or service. If there is a problem with no existing solution, only yours, then you'll be competing against "non-consumption," which means your customers aren't buying anything right now and just kind of suffering along. Alternatively, solutions already exist, but they aren't ideal. In this case, you'll be competing with an existing product or service, and you'll need to show customers how yours is better.

For instance, if you're offering accounting services, you'll need to show how yours meet a need others don't, such as convenience, trustworthiness, or cost effectiveness. If you're building an app to pay for parking, you'll be addressing your customer's need for a way to pay quickly, smoothly, and hassle-free.

2. SOLUTION

The next part of the Lean Canvas is your solution. This is a place to describe the features of your product or service. What will your business do to solve the problem? What are the special qualities of your service or product? You don't need to describe how yours is better—that will come later.

3. CUSTOMER SEGMENTS

Now we move to the Market side of the plan. Who are you trying to sell your product or service to? Try to break it down into the smallest group you can. Is it stay-at-home moms age twenty five to forty? Is it pet owners? Maybe more specifically, dog owners?

List your target customers. Then take it a step further and describe your "first" customers. This is the smallest segment of targeted customers who will be the most interested and easiest to reach. In marketing terms, we call these your "early adopters" or "first adopters." If your target is stay-at-home moms, then your initial segment might be "stay-at-home moms looking for books and crafts for their kids."

This process helps you determine who you want to reach first, then later, and how you'll reach them. It's like concentric circles on an archery target with the bull's-eye at the center. Your market is the whole target. Your first segment is the bull's-eye.

4. UNIQUE VALUE PROPOSITION

This is a place for differentiation. What makes your business different and better? In other words, why you and not the other guy? Here you need to propose the "unique value" of your product or service.

Please don't try to convince yourself that there's no competition, because that's simply not true. Either customers are buying something that helps them solve a problem, or they're buying nothing and you have to compete with non-consumption. It can be difficult to "jumpstart the market." It might work, but it's hard because you have to convince your prospect that they even have a problem in the first place. If that's the case, make sure you test and retest the problem listed in step one.

To identify your unique value proposition, answer the

question: *How does your business solve the customer problem in a way that is different or better than others?*

5. UNFAIR ADVANTAGE

Here you are trying to articulate what parts of your offering are difficult to copy. You might have some new and unique technology or app. You may have special "know-how" to solve a problem and offer a solution.

If you're a "solopreneur" or "lifestyle entrepreneur," you may think this doesn't apply to you. However, you still have to offer something that is difficult to copy. If you're a blogger, author, or producer of info products, your largest unfair advantage is *you*. Your insight and voice cannot be replicated. And, of course, you're probably planning to build an e-mail list. That counts, too!

6. CHANNELS

How will you reach your prospects? Will you sell directly or through middlemen? Are you planning to advertise? Ads can be costly online or offline. Are you hoping customer prospects will find you? In today's Google-centric world, it's possible to have enough search engine optimization (SEO) to position your website high in search results, but this takes time.

In any case, you need to think about and then list the channels by which you'll reach customers.

If you'll be selling a physical product, you have some choices:

you can sell directly to customers through your website or through traditional retailers or distributors. You might sell on Amazon or eBay or a combination of several channels.

If you're developing an app, you can sell through app stores like iTunes and Google Play, and work with partners who will help distribute your app.

7. REVENUE STREAMS

Revenue is the money you generate selling your product or service. You may have more than one product, or you may get perpetual income if you have a subscription business. Depending on your product or service, your customers may be long term, making multiple purchases over time.

These are assumptions you'll want to document, and it's probably time to break out your spreadsheet. Even if you're not an accounting type, you need to create a "back of the envelope" projection of how much money your customers will pay you, and how frequently.

How much money do you plan to charge for your product or service? How many units will a customer buy? This simple sum is an "average order size." The simple formula is: Price × number of units = average order size.

If you estimate the number of times a customer will buy from you *and* when they will stop buying, you can estimate the "lifetime value" of your customer. This is a really important metric because it can help you figure out how much you can spend to acquire your customers.

If you have difficulty estimating your revenue streams, seek out someone in your network who can help. You can also take a "basic financial modeling for entrepreneurs" class. There are a few good ones around, including on Udemy.

8. COST STRUCTURE

Your costs are all the things you're planning to spend money on. It's easy to get overly-detailed in this section, so remember: you don't need to build detailed five-year projections. Try to keep your cost structure to your basic expenses.

You'll want to project the number of staff you need (salaries), your cost to acquire a lead (marketing), your sales expenses to turn prospects into customers (sales), and your rent (unless you're working from home, which is always a good idea in the beginning). If you have a website, you'll have some hosting or development costs. If you're selling a physical product, you'll have the cost of the product itself and the cost to fulfill orders.

If you've never done anything like this before, turn to your network for help, do some research, and learn about it. Ultimately you'll need to understand these numbers, so don't "outsource" this part; learn about it.

You can access a Google spreadsheet template to get you started, along with all the other bonuses for readers, at www.startlaunchgrow.com/nevertoolate-bonuses.

9. KEY METRICS

The goal here is to give you a snapshot into the health of your business. If you can measure it, you'll know how your business is doing, and you can also work to continually improve it.

What aspects are measurable? If you're a blogger, you'll want to know your number of "unique visitors," the number of subscribers, and your "shares" and "likes."

If you're setting up an e-commerce store, you'll want to know your "cost of acquiring a customer" (CAC), your "conversions" (the number of web visitors who end up buying), your "average order size," and your "cost per unit."

In Internet software businesses (called "software as a service" or SaaS), we measure unique visitors, CAC, conversion, "churn" (number of paying customers who leave or stop paying), and "lifetime value" (how much we expect to make from each customer before they churn).

A LIVING DOCUMENT

Your one-page business plan will help you get out into the market, test your assumptions, test your message, and figure out if you have a good business. You should make changes to your plan frequently. Make it a *living document.* In other words, use it as a tool, don't just finish it and leave it on your desk or in Dropbox. Go back and refine it as you learn.

If you go to the Lean Canvas website (LeanStack.com) and read the blog posts, which I recommend, you'll learn about testing each of the nine areas or boxes in your business plan canvas. Your startup journey should be about testing and refining each one. As you do, you develop a more complete and valid picture of how to use your business model.

Remember: knowing your business model and validating your assumptions is critical to growing your company cost-effectively. Think of your initial product, your initial website, your initial ads or blog posts as experiments. Track what works and what doesn't.

DEVELOPING YOUR MVP

If you're building a product or service, you'll want to test the market for it before you spend too much in development or marketing. The best way is by testing with a "minimum viable product," or MVP.

MVP is the smallest amount of a product that will fulfill some of your customer's need *and* allow you to test the market for receptivity.

Eric Reis, the creator of the Lean Startup methodology, defines a minimum viable product as "that version of a new product which allows a team to collect the maximum amount of validated learning about customers with the least amount of effort."

David Mandell took a truly minimal approach when starting PivotDesk. They didn't build anything until they tested the concept with customers:

The way we went from concept to launch is we did everything we could by hand before we built anything. So we literally went door to door with pieces of paper in our hands saying, "Hey, here's what we're doing. Does it work for you?" And if they said yes, I said, "Would you be willing to pay for it?" If they said yes, we said, "Okay, we're going to go do it for you."

We literally did it by hand, and we ran around collecting checks, and walked people from office to office and we did everything we could to test the concept. And once we knew the concept worked, we started building like crazy.

There is both art and science in figuring out what the minimum actually is. Many people think of it incorrectly, stripping away feature after feature until there isn't much left. You need to have compelling features that make customers interested and solve their main problem, just not all of the features you plan to eventually add.

The accompanying graphic is helpful in thinking through what MVP is:

MINIMUM VIABLE PRODUCT

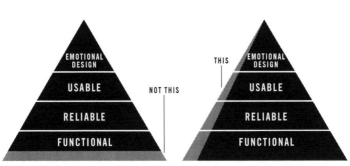

Hat tip to Aarron Walter

If your customer needs to travel from one distant place to another, the product you intend to launch might be a really amazing car. Your MVP wouldn't be just a car engine, no matter how well designed. Your customer can't do much with that except wish it had a body and wheels and a transmission. Your MVP probably isn't a skateboard, because that requires too much work for the customer to travel efficiently. How about a motorcycle or a rickshaw? Or a really basic car with a few cool features to differentiate it? The only way to think through your MVP is by *getting into the market and talking with prospective customers.*

Eric Groves founded Alignable based on ideas he had developed to help small businesses, but he quickly came to understand through talking with customers what they were really interested in:

> We really just went and spent a lot of time with the customers. When we were talking about bringing businesses together, we literally physically brought them together first to see what kind of conversations they were having, what kind of awareness was generated when they did connect with each other. And [as we] did that, [it] opened up opportunities for them to work together on things. We talked to a bunch of them who said, "Really, I love all this notion of a mobile app that would deliver a coupon when someone walks by my store. It sounds really neat, but I'm not interested in it. What I'm really interested in is meeting the guy across the street whose parking lot is always full. How can you use technology to make that happen?"

So, a lot of it was just grassroots, talking to local businesses, and then creating a [basic] product. [Then we] brought it back to those folks...saying, "Does this help?" They reply, "No, no." Okay, well let's get back to the drawing board, do it again.

"Oh yeah, that's kind of cool. Could you do this? Could you do that?" And [we slowly built] out a platform that really made it happen. And we're still going through that process, and talking to customers every day.

In testing your MVP, one of the best assets you bring to bear as a mid-life entrepreneur is your network. You have hundreds of contacts and probably thousands of friends and contacts who can help you discover your market.

Van Barker, founder of outdoor products company YardStash, utilized his network and his years of experience at Hewlett Packard to test his new product:

I did get a lot feedback from the customers. I gave a lot [of units] away, too. I gave probably 50 to 60 of the 200 units away to friends and family in exchange for feedback. So I kind of just made that a marketing expense in 2011. Having the samples was critical.

[Our] product, being something that you stick outdoors year-round...[had] to shed water and rain. A lot of the testing was around its ability to actually withstand the elements and shed water, and also just being easy to set up. So that was kind of the big drive there. And that was born out of [my experience] at HP when you spend hours watching customers take a printer out of a box, and their frustration at setting it up. So a lot of [our testing] was the out-of-box experience, applying it to my own product.

Maybe you come out of a certain industry and you have a great network to solve a problem in that industry. Even if that's not the case, you can find people in your network who can help you get real market feedback on your idea.

EARLY STAGE MARKETING

Once you feel like you have your offering tested with customers and you think it's mostly right, you are going to want to start marketing it. Which method is right for you depends on your business and your budget.

Regardless of which marketing methods you choose, you are going to want to "position" your new product or service. Positioning involves public awareness, perception, and image of a product. You can find out more about positioning in Chapter 8.

Just like your one-page business plan, your positioning is going to change over time. This is because your customers will tell you what they think of your product or service and they will tell you what is unique. Most importantly, they will tell you how they benefit from it, but only if you ask the right questions.

HOW TO PIVOT

Many times it happens that your original idea simply isn't resonating with your customers. It can be incredibly difficult to face, because you put so much work into generating the idea and bringing your MVP to market. If this happens, take a step back. Sometimes, though rarely, your idea is so brilliant and ahead of its time that the market just isn't ready for it.

It's more likely that you missed on defining the customer's problem or your solution to it. A lot of times you *think* the customer has a huge problem, but when you get to talking with them, you find out that it just isn't that big an issue.

This is where the idea of the "pivot" comes in. The term comes from basketball. In basketball, it means keeping one foot firmly on the ground and picking up your other foot to turn your body. You can turn in any direction, as long as you keep your pivot foot down.

In the startup realm, it means changing direction, but still keeping some elements of your original business or concept. You don't need to scrap everything. You might just need to make some tweaks, either going after a slightly different problem or using a different solution.

Some pretty amazing, giant companies have been built on a pivot from the original idea.

In 2007, Andrew Mason founded a business called The Point, a social media platform to help people solve social issues by aggregating people with like interests. It was assumed that enough people would reach a "tipping point," hence the name The Point. After a year, this business really didn't go anywhere. Investor Eric Lefkofsky suggested that the business could be repurposed to help people save money through "group buying." The founders experimented with this new idea and the "group coupon," or Groupon, was born.[30]

If your initial idea isn't resonating, isn't attracting attention, if it isn't actually solving the customer's pain, don't be afraid to re-evaluate. It might not mean that you need to quit, but rather that you need to pivot.

You now have the basics of a business plan and you're on your way to positioning your product or service. You're gearing up to launch your business, so let's take a deeper look into marketing.

MARKETING YOUR STARTUP

---

*"Our job is to connect to people, to
interact with them in a way that leaves
them better than we found them, more
able to get where they'd like to go."*

SETH GODIN, AUTHOR AND ENTREPRENEUR

Growing revenue for your startup requires you to put together
a plan to market and sell. If you come out of sales, or you
have some general management experience, this may seem
routine. If you're new to marketing and your experience is in
other functions, then you have some important things to learn.

Regardless of your background, selling and marketing in a
startup are fundamentally different than in a large company.
It's basically the difference between "gorilla" and "guerilla."
Big companies use "gorilla marketing" to assert their power
to beat smaller competitors. It means using mass media,

spending lots of money, and making a big splash to get consumers to take notice and try their product.

Startups use "guerilla marketing" to nimbly engage pockets of potential buyers. By targeting a narrow niche of prospects, you can get your message to them inexpensively. Guerilla marketing encourages word-of-mouth marketing through web content and consumer testimonials. These tactics help drive people to your website to learn more about your products. Guerilla marketing is also about emphasizing solutions to customer problems that existing businesses do not offer.

WHAT'S YOUR BUSINESS MODEL?

There is no universal way to market your company. Every startup is different and every founder's goals are different.

Your company may need to market business-to-business (B2B), business-to-consumer (B2C), or locally, nationally, or internationally. It could be targeting a particular industry, or it could be applicable across most industries.

What are your goals for your business?

Some founders are trying to grow as large as possible as fast as possible. You're probably thinking, *Well, who doesn't want that?* But the truth is that many founders these days are looking for businesses that are more portable and can be run from anywhere. They want a business that meets their lifestyle. Freedom-oriented businesses grow a bit more slowly, because the founders generally don't want full time employees and don't want to raise investment capital for sales and marketing.

WHAT'S YOUR NICHE?

Regardless of your goals for the business, you need to identify and locate your first customers. You need to find a small niche of initial buyers. This is best accomplished through "positioning." Positioning is a marketing term used to describe the process of figuring out who your target customers are, how your product makes them feel, and how it differs from other products.

Think about how you feel about Apple or Starbucks, or about the best car you ever owned. Then think about how you feel about your cable company. Probably not as warm and fuzzy.

The best brands develop an emotional connection with their customers. Successful companies and brands carefully *position* themselves with customers so that their products and messages resonate on an emotional level.

Positioning is not about writing taglines or great ads. It's about narrowing down your audience to the smaller slices you want, determining how your offering is different from others, and describing what benefits you offer your customers. Even if your new business is a blog or a book, positioning helps you find your unique voice for your unique audience.

YOUR POSITIONING STATEMENT

In his best-selling marketing book *Crossing the Chasm,* author and marketer Geoffrey Moore promotes a simple format for positioning:

- **For** (target customers)
- **Who** (have the following problem)
- **Our product is a** (describe the product or solution)
- **That provides** (cite the breakthrough capability)
- **Unlike** (reference competition)
- **Our product/solution** (describe the key point of competitive differentiation)

Here's an example of a Geoffrey- Moore-style "positioning statement" for Lexus:

For affluent drivers who seek luxury vehicles of the highest quality and reliability, Lexus constantly pursues the finest materials, the best technologies, and the ultimate in quality control to ensure the perfect luxury vehicle experience.

A good positioning statement starts with defining your target customers. Is your product or service for pet owners, bloggers, college-age women, or stay-at-home moms?

Understanding the demographics of your target customers (the "who" in your positioning statement) is essential. In order to best reach your audience, you can segment them further. Focus on your prospects' concerns, dreams, and problems. What are the issues they face? What problems do they need to solve? You are trying to determine your customer niche.

Seth Godin, marketer and author of *Tribes* and *Linchpin*,

asks the following questions in his blog post, "Who Are Your Customers?":

- What do they believe?
- Who do they trust?
- What are they afraid of?
- Who do they love?
- What are they seeking?

To really understand your potential customer, you might also ask: What do they dream about? What keeps them up at night? What motivates them? Remember: you want to encourage an emotional connection in your customer to your product.

It helps if you narrow your niche audience as much as possible. First-time founders often worry about defining their niche too narrowly. They want to appeal to as wide an audience as possible. You can be explicit, however, without being exclusive. By serving your niche audience well and addressing their problems, other consumers will find you, too.

The "our product" part of positioning explains the product features, as in "the Dyson vacuum is a lightweight, easy-to-maneuver vacuum cleaner that never loses suction."

Importantly, a positioning statement is not a tag line. For example, Nike's positioning is about inspiring the athlete in all of us. Their tag line is "Just Do It." One may lead to the other, but they are not the same thing. At this point, you don't really need to worry about tag lines. You do, however, need to create a positioning statement to establish your place in a customer's awareness.

DIFFERENTIATION

A good positioning statement describes how the product is different from others. This is important because it establishes the value of a product. For the Dyson vacuum, the fact that it doesn't lose suction is a huge differentiator. It's the reason Sir James Dyson built the product in the first place. That's what made it different from Hoover and Bissell.

If you're offering a product, you state the major differences between your product and the alternatives. Why will customers choose your product over the alternatives? Is it because of particular features? A lower price? Ease of use? If you are going after an established market, your product will need to be substantially better than the alternative, perhaps as much as ten times better, to get customers to switch.

BENEFITS

Every good positioning statement focuses on the benefits of the product, not just the features. Products that focus on features often struggle to stay relevant because some other company comes out with a better feature, like a bigger engine (cars), a brighter screen (computers), or a longer battery life (cell phones).

Spelling out the benefits of your product and appealing to consumer desire for those benefits generates consumer emotion. A benefit could be real—such as more time, more money, less effort, greater safety—or it could be perceived. An example of a perceived benefit is the "cool factor" of certain products, like iPhones. The reason Apple devotees wait in line for the new iPhone is because owning the latest iPhone makes those buyers feel cool.

Try to speak to a customer's hopes and aspirations. How will they benefit from your product or service? How will you help them solve their problem?

Blogger Jon Morrow suggests that bloggers think about potential readers like the "walking dead." You have to attach jumper cables to them by tapping into their fears, dreams, desires, and hatreds. You can think of your consumers in the same way. If you can establish that emotional connection, the walking dead come alive.

MARKETING BY WORD OF MOUTH

As you know well by now, one of your advantages as a mid-life entrepreneur is your social network. You can put it to work for you in marketing by asking your friends and colleagues to spread the word about your product or service. If they know potential customers, see if they will make introductions for you.

Testimonials are fantastic to help convince new buyers that your product is of high quality. Social proof matters, so get your network of friends and colleagues to provide testimonials.

Social media is a great way to leverage your network. If you add up all of your first-, second-, and third-degree social connections, they could easily total in the hundreds of thousands. Use that to your advantage. Your connections can spread the word by "like," "share," "tweet," and other pathways.

MARKETING ONLINE

There are legions of tools, consultants, and agencies that want a piece of your marketing attention and budget. Even if you have a great marketer working for you, you'll need to make difficult prioritization decisions because of limited resources. Learning about digital and offline marketing venues and tools is the key to successful marketing.

Your Website: No matter what type of business you run, from a yoga studio to a tech company to a food business, you're going to want a professional website. Most consumers start their buying online and this is the first interaction they'll have with your company.

It's easier than ever to build a basic professional website. You'll need to purchase a domain name and use a hosting service. Website templates are readily available at WordPress with customizable themes.

E-mail: Once you have a domain and website, you can get your own inexpensive, professional-looking e-mail alias, such as you@yourcompany.com, through Gmail or your hosting provider.

Most new companies establish relationships with prospects via e-mail. For this you'll need an e-mail service provider (ESP) to capture and maintain customer e-mails to communicate your messages. There are many easy-to-use services like Constant Contact, MailChimp, or AWeber. They have easy-to-set-up forms to facilitate e-mail flow right from your site to the ESP.

Logo: Some people believe that a logo is really important and worth spending a lot of money on. Personally, I think you will probably change your logo (and even your business name) over time, so you should not spend too much on a logo. There are super-cheap options like Fiverr ($5) and slightly more expensive options like 99Designs, where multiple designers submit logo designs ($299). Of course, you can also hire a professional designer and spend thousands.

Landing Pages: A landing page is a dedicated webpage that welcomes visitors and directs customer flow. It can help begin a customer relationship, collect an e-mail address, or provide additional information about a prospect.

As a small business, you typically offer something of value in exchange for an e-mail, phone number, or even a click. This could be a white paper about your solution, the first chapter of a book, an interview you've done, or a free test of your product.

It used to be the case that you had to know design and coding to set these up. Today, through inexpensive services like Lead-Pages (www.leadpages.net) or Instapage (www.instapage.com), you can set up professional-looking landing pages in a matter of minutes. They can either be hosted by the service or on your WordPress or Tumblr site. Landing pages can integrate seamlessly with your e-mail service provider.

Advertising: Once you have a website and landing page, you may want to begin running some small-scale advertising. The most popular platforms of online advertising are Google Adwords, Bing (Microsoft), and Facebook, but there are many others, including Twitter, Pinterest, LinkedIn, and Outbrain.

These are called pay-per-click (PPC) ad platforms because you only pay when the viewer clicks on your ad and lands on your homepage or landing page. This is quite different than running a newspaper ad or even display advertising on the Internet where you are paying for the number of people who view the ad, not the number of people who click on it.

The great thing about these platforms is that they enable you to target your niche prospects with pretty amazing accuracy. Think of all the things that Facebook knows about you: your sex, age, location, the language you speak, your hobbies, the pages you like, your work. You can target by any or all of these. On Google, targeting works differently: you select keywords that people are using as search terms.

With a very small budget, less than $10 per day, you can get going with these platforms. In addition to setting your daily or weekly budget, you also decide how much you are willing to spend for each click. You can spend a lot per click in the beginning and ratchet that down over time to a level that is more profitable for your company. However, it's easy to waste money if you don't know anything about pay-per-click advertising, so research the subject or take an online course to find out more. It's fairly easy to come up to speed on the basics.

MARKETING CONTENT THAT PEOPLE WANT

The idea of *content marketing* or "strategic marketing" is not new, but it has grown significantly in popularity as a result of new trends.

One trend is the decline of "interruption marketing." This is a pejorative term first coined by marketer and author Seth Godin to describe sales tactics and marketing methods that distract the potential buyer from what they are doing.

For instance, direct mail in the form of sales letters and post-cards is an intrusion on a person's home or office. There's been a steep decline in response rates to direct mail since the early 1990s. Consumers are increasingly annoyed by this type of intrusion.

As direct mail effectiveness declined, marketers turned to e-mail. Hundreds of billions of unwanted e-mails, or "spam," flooded our in-boxes until we collectively had enough. Congress passed the CAN-SPAM law in 2003, making it illegal to send unsolicited e-mail. Don't get me wrong—e-mail is still an incredible marketing tool. It's just that you can no longer buy lists and send out bulk e-mails.

The ultimate "interruption marketing" tactic is the cold call. You're sitting doing some work and the phone rings. You look at the caller ID, decide you don't recognize the number, and don't pick up. Since the rollout of caller ID and the ubiquity of voicemail, we can now ignore unwanted phone calls.

MARKETING AS SOCIAL RELATIONSHIP

The opposite of interruption marketing is *permission marketing*. Permission marketing is where your business is part of the buyer's path of education. Your business gets permission to deliver timely, targeted, relevant messages in some form. You get that permission either because the prospect is seeking information or they have opted-in to an e-mail list.

The consumer has agreed to receive marketing content they consider valuable and relevant to their lives and interests.

According to Godin: "Permission is like dating. You don't start by asking for the sale at first impression. You earn the right, over time, bit by bit."[31]

Instead of thrusting your message at people who may not want it, content marketing methods, also called "inbound marketing," are aimed at helping prospects find you. Content marketing involves creating content in whatever form that will engage prospects in their buying journey. The content could be a blog post, an article in a major publication, a YouTube video describing how to do something (and using your product), a Vine, you name it.

The idea is that prospects are using Google, YouTube, and other social methods to search for answers to their problems. You create content hoping to generate their interest so that you can be found. Realistically, your content probably won't lead to an instantaneous purchase transaction. It is the beginning of a relationship.

Think of your own patterns of buying new products. You probably start with Google, Amazon, or social media. You ask around. You research products and companies. Good content can help you on that buying journey.

The advantages of permission-based marketing are that messages can be targeted to a specific consumer or niche. You are not broadcasting your message to "anyone and everyone," but rather to small pockets of consumers who have a challenge and are looking for a solution. This can be much more cost effective than broad-based mass marketing.

Two new concepts you'll want to learn and embrace as you begin marketing your products are "buying funnel" and "conversion rate."

A *buying funnel* refers to the journey that buyers take along the buying process. You want to define different stages and treat your prospects differently along those stages.

Conversion rate is the rate at which a given group of prospects moves to the next stage of your funnel. For example, you write a blog post with the goal of bringing traffic to your website. It isn't likely that someone will move straight from reading a blog post to buying, so you want to capture their e-mail address on your blog page. In this example, your conversion rate is the percentage of readers who give you their e-mail.

Managing and optimizing your conversion rates for different points on your funnel is one of the most important levers you have to turn browsers into buyers over time.

Marketing is increasingly relationship-based, which explains the popularity of content-based, permission-based marketing.

They empower both you and the customer to begin forming a long-term relationship. The most profitable businesses acquire customers once and see them return for purchases over time. This is a much better scenario than needing to acquire your customers over and over.

GROWTH HACKING

The term "growth hacking" was coined by marketer Sean Ellis to refer to strategies, tips, and tricks employed by some of the world's fastest growing companies. These companies built growth levers right into their products by integrating product development and marketing, and using all the data available through the Internet.

Examples of growth hacking include Hotmail's use of "Get your free e-mail at Hotmail" in the signature line of all e-mails, Dropbox offering free storage to anyone who referred a friend (advertised in the product and in the setup process), Airbnb getting all of their listings to automatically appear on Craigslist, and Twitter recommending five people for you to follow during the setup phase of your account.

All of these examples are ones in which the product team and marketing team designed the product with growth in mind. They worked together to increase the number of people who would sign up for a new product, and to increase the chance that they would quickly get value and remain a user.

Adopting growth hacking methodologies for your startup means iterating very quickly on the product design, development, and marketing cycles of your company. Your designers, product, and marketing teams need to work closely together to make sure that growth is the number one priority. They need to make setup and use incredibly easy and build hooks directly into the product.

Even if you're not a marketing expert, you can learn the basics of bringing your product or service to market. As you've seen, marketing isn't nearly as complex and expensive as many people think it is.

FUNDING YOUR BUSINESS

---

*"To guarantee success, act as if
it were impossible to fail."*

DOROTHEA BRANDE, AUTHOR

Entrepreneurs often think they should raise money in order to quit their job, start their company, and grow their business. However, this isn't how it works. Investors don't just give money to founders because they have a good startup idea.

Investors fund companies that have identified a need, spoken with customers, and built an initial product or service to fulfill their need. We identified this process in Chapter 7 as finding "product/market fit," and investors typically are looking to fund businesses that have already found it.

If you've already built your product and found customers, you might feel you don't need funding. Maybe you don't. Many successful businesses don't need outside investment. You might prefer to bootstrap your way to success.

But it's also possible you'll need capital to build a better product or a second product. Or perhaps you want to grow your business very fast and invest in salespeople and marketing. Or you need to invest in inventory to grow your e-commerce business. Any of these goals might require external capital.

Capital might be crucial to your business success, so it's crucial to know how to find sources and raise necessary funds.

Conversations with entrepreneurs often turn to capital. Most young companies are undercapitalized, though capital is the lifeblood of a growing business. Businesses need capital to grow because everything from sales to marketing to inventory require capital in advance of generating revenue. Cash flows often lag revenue, except in rare cases.

The Kauffman Foundation, one of the leading sources of information about entrepreneurship in the United States, studied the sources of capital of *Inc.* magazine's 5,000 fastest growing companies.[32] The study revealed that only 14 percent of entrepreneurs on the list used no financing. All the others had used personal savings or raised money from banks, friends, angel investors, or venture capitalists.

It is possible to build a business without external capital, but it's challenging to build a big or fast-growing business in this way. Depending on your business, you will likely need capital to fund the development of your product or your cash flow needs as the business starts to grow.

A fairly common pattern is to self-fund, or bootstrap, the business while in the formative stages of generating, developing, and testing your idea. When the business starts to add customers and employees, founders find they need some outside capital. It's still early in the game, so a small amount is raised. In this way the founder maintains primary ownership and control.

BOOTSTRAPPING

Almost all businesses are bootstrapped for a period of time.

Bootstrapping is the process of funding your business yourself without outside investors. Even if you think you're going to need outside investment, you will probably need to bootstrap your business for some length of time. Why? For two good reasons:

1. Investors are reluctant to put money into a business unless you are working on it full time and have made significant progress.
2. The more progress you make before you raise capital, the higher investors will value your company. When you do raise money, you'll be giving up less of your business to your investors. If you ever sell the business, or it starts generating significant cash, more of it will belong to you.

There are several ways to bootstrap a new company. You can use your savings to invest in the business and pay your expenses until the company is large enough to fund itself, and then raise outside capital. This requires significant savings, especially for mid-life entrepreneurs who have higher expenses at their stage of life. It's not as if you can eat Ramen noodles and crash on your friend's sofa anymore. You probably have a mortgage, car payments, kids to feed and clothe, and college and retirement savings to fund.

Many of the entrepreneurs I interviewed had the savings they needed. A few had been part of successful companies that had generated a level of wealth. They bootstrapped their companies for as long as a year before they turned to outside investors.

When Sara Schaer left Snapfish to found KangaDo, she was able to bootstrap her company:

> We bootstrapped it for over a year. I'd say maybe a year and a half...and then we pitched it to 500 Startups.

> Certainly not being in it alone [author's note: having a spouse] and not having to worry about my own healthcare and [other] costs for that type of thing helped immensely. The addition of two kids [added expenses]. Kids are expensive, so I think looking back, I don't think I could have done this really, or bootstrapped it for as long as we did, without having another breadwinner in the household... It's definitely an advantage for folks not having to do it all by themselves, but you can get away with delaying the fundraising a bit longer.

Even if you don't have significant savings, you can still

bootstrap your company by starting as a side business and building it up while you're still working. The progress you make on the side, proving your assumptions and getting a basic product out, will go a long way toward convincing investors to put money in.

You might also be able to generate enough revenue so that you can quit your job and partly or entirely replace the income from your day job.

Van Barker, founder of Yardstash, did exactly that:

> When I quit [my day job], I think I had about a quarter million in revenue, and about $70,000 in net profit. Before that I was working full time, and I was running to the stairwell [of my old company to take calls related to YardStash], and [it felt like] I was basically having an affair with my company... It just didn't seem to be ethical anymore to be managing a team of people that depended on me, and also running a small company on the side.

> The short answer is that when I quit, it was profitable. So I could see that if I could ramp volume that there'd be money coming in. I didn't see [a case where] I would have to actually write a check and take a risk on that side. So worst case would be, income zero, but not negative. That was my simple math.

> I think by virtue of selling directly one-on-one to customers, I could see that I could sell two, four, five [units] a day, even if I just went out to swap meets or sold them out of the back of my van down by the river. So, if I needed to sell units, I had something physical that I could actually get $100 for, and it would

just be a matter of how much I wanted to hustle.

It made it less daunting for me, because I could...just sell two or three a day versus *I've got to land a big fish*. It was more the virtue of the business model of going direct to consumer.

Fortunately, in 2012, I was part of another smaller company that was bought in late 2011. So I had gotten some money from the acquisition...[and] I just rolled some of that into [procuring] the inventory. And that's part of the journey, too, in that there was kind of a liquidity event in my day job that helped to give more of a cushion to launch YardStash. So I could use that cash to fund the inventory out the gate. But I haven't had to do any fundraising.

I think I could continue to bootstrap it at the current rate. Keeping in mind, it's like a $500,000 to $600,000 company right now. So, obviously, if I want to take it to the next level, I think I'd have to raise some capital for that, but for now I think I will still bootstrap it.

SOURCES OF CAPITAL

When you decide to complete the bootstrapping phase and start looking for capital, you can find it available from several sources.

FRIENDS AND FAMILY

Raising money from friends and family can involve a formal pitch and investment documents or simply an informal conversation. People who know you well and trust you might be happy to invest in your company because they believe in you and your vision.

Friends and family investors are great to turn to early in the development of your new business. They will often need less convincing about the product idea or the market.

One of the challenges, however, is it can be difficult to set a valuation for the business. Friends and family members are not professional investors and will not have a good sense of how to value a startup. Equally important, you don't want to set a sky-high value and be unfair to these first investors.

Eric Groves and Venkat Krishnamurthy, the founders of Alignable, raised small amounts from family and friends before pursuing seed money more formally:

> Well, we did bootstrap it. Both Venkat and I were fairly fortunate in the successes we'd had in the past... We could basically go a year without drawing a salary and we brought on board one developer. Then we raised some money from friends and family in small amounts, but we kept our burn down to basically nothing while we built out our first iteration of the product just to prove that the market was there. And then, once we had that, then we went out and raised a little bit more seed money...from a variety of folks...[such as] CrunchFund on the West Coast, and on the East Coast it was Longwood Ventures, NextView, and a couple other local Boston individuals.

They're all connections that we'd had in the past, who looked at us and said, "Well, here are two seasoned execs of companies that have done this before; seem to be looking at a pretty interesting opportunity." And, so, you know, we raised a little over a million dollars that way and that really helped us get the product to market. And then last March we did a more traditional Series A raise.

ANGELS, ANGEL GROUPS, AND ANGEL PLATFORMS

Angels are wealthy individuals who regularly invest in startup companies. You can meet angels in all sorts of professional and personal settings. You'll be surprised at the number of people who might be willing to invest in your business when you start looking for money.

Angel investors often get together in "angel groups" so they can pool their money, share in the due diligence of vetting a new investment, get a broader perspective on the merits of an investment, and for social reasons.

Pitching an angel group can be a lot like pitching a venture capital firm. There will be multiple decision makers. You'll have a limited amount of time to pitch before a Q&A session. It can be a little nerve wracking, but with practice, you can do fine.

One recent trend in angel investing is the growth in "angel platforms." These are technology websites that list both companies and angels interested in looking for investment opportunities. These angel platforms are like eBay or even Match for angels and startups. They can be a great way to meet new angels and raise additional funds over and above what you can generate from personal networking. The largest of these is Angel List (www.angel.co). If you are interested in raising angel capital, you probably want to list your company there.

VENTURE CAPITALISTS

Venture capitalists (VCs) are professional investors whose job is to invest in startups. They raise money from pension funds and college endowments and hope to return many times that amount back to their investors.

VCs are generally looking for large companies. They want moonshots. So if you go in with a solid growth business, they often aren't interested. It isn't that yours is a bad business or unworthy of investment; it's simply that their parameters are different.

The biggest challenge for a mid-life entrepreneur in regard to venture capitalists is age and profile. VCs often follow popular patterns, so if they see a mobile messaging company founded by recent college grads, they're going to look for more of those. Many of the most successful recent multi-billion-dollar companies—Google, Facebook, YouTube, Tumblr, Instagram—were started by young entrepreneurs. This is the model VCs are now chasing for "winning investments."

Though this bias among VCs for younger entrepreneurs exists, you can overcome the bias. David Mandell, founder of Pivot-Desk, puts it pretty succinctly:

If you look at the VC community in general, I would say yes, I think they are absolutely skewed towards younger entrepreneurs because they have an image of success in their brains that the media and everyone else portrays, so they make decisions based on those images that they've seen. Now, the reality is if you find the right investor for what you're doing and for you as a person, I find that age doesn't really matter. In fact, a lot of times it can be a benefit.

Sara Schaer saw this bias firsthand when she went to raise capital:

People ask me about the ageism and ask about the disadvantage to being a female founder [and] mom founder. Nobody comes out and says, "You're too old," obviously. However, I have been made aware by what I would consider friendly investors, "Hey, you should be aware—you don't either look or sound like the Mark Zuckerbergs of the world."

This person was even very explicit. He said, "Look, I think you have your act together. You're very thoughtful and you have answers to all my questions, but you've got to realize that investors are looking for a pattern. That pattern doesn't look like you. There aren't very many people who look and sound like you who have made it very big." Investors are asking, "What do founders look like who have hit it out of the park and made a lot of money?"

And he said, "I'll take a bet on you guys because I believe in you and I believe in this problem and you obviously have a track record. But just so you know, that's what you are up against." I think this person literally said, "You have the answers for all my questions, but you should know that these twenty-somethings who come in who are super overconfident and don't know the answers to the questions, but who are so arrogant that somehow you come out of there thinking that they are going to figure [it] out, just because of their attitude." That's what you need to realize that you are up against. You need to target investors that think differently or you need to figure out how to play that game the way everyone else is playing it.

I think that with this product it is definitely a question of 1) Targeting the right investors. Have they invested in the space? Are they in the 500 Startups network? Leveraging all the credentials that we have, whether that's our track record, whether it is prior investors, are they affiliated or do they often co-invest with 500 Startups or Structure Capital? 2) Are they parents themselves? Do they have other [similar] family-focused companies in their portfolio? Are there other connections that we have through prior professional friends or colleagues in common? Any kind of affiliation or analogous behavior?

And the other way is, frankly, to work on projecting confidence. Look, you've come this far. So many startups die even before getting off the ground. So many things can happen—cofounders fall out, somebody else blows you out of the space by doing something ten times better for free. Facebook or Google offers something to the planet that you have been trying to do, so game over. So just really projecting the confidence that not only do you have the right problem, but you are the right person to solve it. And just really not leaving any kind of self-doubt visible at all, because that goes to the [investor's] pattern matching.

It's a great exercise and I think it's something that 500 Startups was an extremely great training ground for, in terms of the pitch practice, storytelling, and just being excellent in delivery and really, really solid on your business and knowing where you are and where your head is. To out-perform on your pitch.

Really, the Holy Grail is that traction is the greatest equalizer. So if you can excel at your business, all of these other biases tend to fall away. If you're knocking it out of the park, then it's a lot less important what you look like or how old you are. So try to get there as quickly as you possibly can.

Jack O'Toole founded FreshAir Sensor Corp. after twenty five years in the military. Following his military career, he decided to get his MBA at the Tuck School of Business at Dartmouth College. There he met his cofounder, Joe BelBruno, a Dartmouth professor of chemistry. The pair co-founded FreshAir Sensor based on BelBruno's research into novel polymer chemistry. I spoke with them about their journey. They shared Sara Schaer's perspective on the challenges of raising outside capital as a mid-life entrepreneur:

BelBruno: I think, well, I've talked to a couple [of investors] who have said that their preferred founder is like twenty five and lives in his parents' basement.

O'Toole: That's what they prefer to invest in. Honestly, though, in talking to the people we got money from, I think they were more comfortable [with us] because I was closer in age to them. They felt like, "Jack has run things before, he knows what's going on, and he's not going to do anything crazy and blow it."

Vivek Wadhwa, Stanford University professor and author of the Kauffman Foundation study on older entrepreneurs, was pretty blunt in his assessment of venture capital as it relates to older founders:

> There is a very strong VC bias [toward younger founders]. It is one reason why the VC system itself is in trouble. VC is becoming less and less relevant to innovation.
>
> The power is shifting. It used to be in the Valley that when you met a VC, he was like a god you bowed down to. Now the VCs are sucking up to entrepreneurs because they're worried about missing out on the next big deal.
>
> Also, if you look at the returns, look at the Kauffman data on the returns that venture capital is producing. The returns are dismal.
>
> As a whole, the VC system has been biased. Their assumptions have been flawed and they are paying for it.
>
> The rules of the game have changed dramatically because the cost of starting a company has dropped exponentially. You don't need venture capital to start a technology company anymore. You did years ago, because you needed racks of servers, you needed expensive computers and storage. All of this is practically free right now. You get unlimited computing on the web and scale up as you go. The costs of starting a company have dropped dramatically. You can build lots of new technologies without requiring millions of dollars of venture capital.
>
> My advice to the older workers, and to women, is screw the

venture capitalists. Just bypass them. Go and build it, and they'll come.

I receive messages practically every other day from people who have achieved extraordinary success and did it without venture capital. I was literally responding to one twenty minutes ago. These are the types of e-mails I get all the time. People who defy the odds and achieve success.

BANKS

My personal opinion is that bank loans are not commonly a ready source of capital for most startups unless you are buying an existing small business that has revenue and cash flow. Most banks ask for one to three years of prior financial statements for your company before they make a loan, and they usually require the business to be cash-flow positive. This is because a company that is losing money is riskier to them in terms of paying back the loan. Unlike angels and VCs, banks are not in the business of taking much risk.

Bank funding is possible if you have been running your startup as a side business to your day job for a few years. You might have achieved some profits and have enough business history to get a loan.

Interestingly, the Kauffman Foundation shows that more than half of *Inc.* magazine's 5,000 fastest growing companies have used bank loans to fund their businesses. This runs counter to my experience, though perhaps this study reflects high-growth businesses that were more mature at the point they raised bank financing.

Since you have a couple of decades of experience, you might have a network that includes some local bankers. Talk to them and see what their requirements are. But don't expect a positive response, at least not until your company is a little more mature. It could also be the case that the banks will ask for some form of personal collateral, like your home equity or 401(k) savings, before funding your business.

PAYBACK: DELIVERING RETURN ON INVESTMENT

There are significant pros and cons to each source of capital or bootstrapping exclusively. The bottom line is, the more money you raise, the less control you will have over your business.

First and foremost, investors demand a return on their money. There are only a few ways to get a return. The most common is to sell the business. If you sell for a high enough price, your investors will get a substantial return.

A less common but equally lucrative way to pay back your investors is to take your company public in an Initial Public Offering, or IPO. There are two reasons this is less common. The first is that businesses need to get to a sufficient size with predictable revenue and earnings in order to go public. The second reason is that regulations imposed on public companies coupled with the demands of public investors can make it not much fun to run a public company.

Another way to deliver returns to your investors is to pay them back in the form of dividends. If you believe that you can be very profitable and deliver significant dividends to your investors, then you might be able to negotiate this kind of model.

The tradeoff with taking on some kind of debt is that it has to be paid back with interest, usually on a regular schedule. This can be challenging in a small business where things can be unpredictable. You might have a bad month or a bad quarter and be unable to make your debt payments. This can put you in default of your loan and your debt holders could take control of your business.

HOW MUCH FUNDING DO YOU NEED?

One of the hardest parts of preparing for fundraising is figuring out how much money you should raise. It's tricky. Raise too little and your company may go out of business because you don't have enough cash. Raise too much and you will suffer significant dilution (the amount of the business you have to give up to your investors) at the early stage.

It's time to get your spreadsheet out and do some projections. If your spreadsheet skills are poor, you should take a little time to improve them. Being intimate with the numbers of your business is not only key to raising funds, but also to operating and scaling the company successfully. You can call on friends or professionals to help here, but be sure you "own" the numbers and don't outsource the thinking.

There are a few mistakes to avoid. The first is being overly detailed. In my work advising startups, I sometimes see projections month by month going out five years with line items for everything. Trust me, you aren't going to spend very much on office supplies, so you don't need that much detail.

I would suggest creating monthly or quarterly projections for twenty four months and then annually after that. You're really only trying to figure out how much capital you need *now* and what you're going to use it for.

DOING PROJECTIONS

Make sure you have projections for three different expense-related categories, or "buckets."

1. ASSUMPTIONS

Your first expense bucket is your assumptions. The good thing about spreadsheets is that changing your assumptions changes the whole model. You should build your financial model to allow for change. So if you need help with spreadsheets, make sure you get it.

Your assumptions, or *inputs,* will be things like the number of units you sell, marketing costs like Google Adwords, price per unit sold, number of sales each salesperson can make, and technology and support costs (if you're building a tech company).

Your assumptions might change over time in your model. As an example, the productivity of a salesperson, even after they ramp up, might improve in the second year as the product becomes better known and you have some customer references. Similarly, your cost of marketing might go down as you get better leading customers through a trial.

2. MAJOR EXPENSES

The second bucket is major expenses. Some founders go crazy here with detail, which isn't necessary. The major things to include are personnel costs, rent, tech and office supplies, travel, marketing, manufacturing costs, and sales commissions.

3. REVENUE

The third bucket is revenue. It's important here to project the number of units you're going to sell, not just the total revenue, so that you can allow for changes in your price per unit. It's also important to tie your expenses to your revenue. In other words, some of your expenses, like marketing and sales, drive the revenue that you will produce.

YOUR BUSINESS MODEL

One of the most important parts of this exercise is to play around with your business model to see what parts really drive it. In other words, you should understand how to make your company grow like crazy. On the flipside, you should understand which assumptions will tank the business if they don't come true.

For an Internet company, one of the crucial metrics is "conversion." Not only do you need lots of traffic to come to your site, but you need it to convert visitors into users. So the conversion assumptions in your model, and how they play out once you start testing, are one of the most important levers for this type of company.

You will have your own levers for making your business successful. You will want to know those, and investors will want to know them, too.

Even if you're a blogger planning to offer info products, or a solopreneur with a simple e-commerce business model, an evolving plan is important. You are running an Internet business, just on a smaller scale. Once you're established, you may still want or need some outside capital to help fund inventory or to introduce new products.

HOW TO APPROACH INVESTORS

DO YOUR RESEARCH

The first step to approaching investors is to know which investors you want. You may be thinking *I just need capital, I don't care who my investors are*, but that's shortsighted.

First, investors become partners in your business. Even though you'll continue to control the business, your investors will have a say in how things are run. Very often they will demand a seat on the company's board of directors. They will be key players if you go to raise a second round of financing.

Second, most investors invest in certain types of companies.

If you're raising money for a restaurant chain, you can't approach investors who invest in Internet companies or health care. It would be a waste of your time and a waste of theirs. So take the time to find the right investors by doing your research upfront.

As you get a little further along in the process, you are going to want to do reference checks on the investors around the same time they start researching you. You can find out a lot about the way the investor acts when things go poorly, or when it is time to sell the company. Try to find other entrepreneurs who have worked with that investor, and listen to them. If you're approaching VCs rather than angels, you want to find out about the partner who will work with you, not just the fund.

Most of the time, you don't want to go in cold to an investor. You want to get a warm introduction from someone they know, like another entrepreneur they have backed or a lawyer they work with.

Investors receive hundreds or even thousands of pitches from new entrepreneurs every year. Going in cold usually gets your e-mail ignored or presentation (your "pitch deck") put at the bottom of the pile. If you get an intro from someone they respect, you will at least get a thoughtful review of your idea and perhaps a meeting.

The best introductions to VCs are from other entrepreneurs whom they have funded or know well. So you should start the process of developing your network with as many other entrepreneurs as you can. The next best sources are other professionals with whom they work, like lawyers and other service providers.

Also, sometimes it makes sense to start building a relationship beforehand. Some investors like to meet you and monitor the progress you are making as part of considering an investment. That's fine, as long as you approach it the same way.

Mark Suster, founder of Upfront Ventures and former high-tech CEO, describes it this way in his fantastic blog, "Both Sides of the Table":

> Remember that most fundraising takes time. It's about building long-term relationships and showing traction over time.
>
> Let's be honest. This is not unlike a major biz dev deal you're trying to sign or a big sales campaign into the VP of a major company. I like to tell entrepreneurs to treat it like a sales campaign—*exactly* like a sales campaign. You would never go see an important executive at a customer and then sit around and wait for them to realize how great you are.
>
> I am really surprised how many entrepreneurs pitch me and then I never hear from them again. I guess they assume that since I didn't e-mail or call I must not be interested. This isn't always the case.[33]

YOUR INVESTOR PITCH

There are many different opinions about the content of an investor pitch. There is no exactly right way to do it. The best pitch is the one you can give really well.

My general opinion is that entrepreneurs try to do too much with their pitch. They are often too long, too detailed, and the pitch doesn't explain their vision or passion for the company.

Basically, your presentation, called a "pitch deck," should include:

- The problem the market faces (use stories and anecdotes to make this feel personal).
- Your solution.
- The market opportunity (size).
- Your team.
- Your traction (product, customers).
- Your business model (how you are going to make money).
- Your strategy (and approach to growing the business).
- Investment (how much are you raising, and where it will go).
- Your planned milestones.

One of the best places to see great pitch decks is at www.pitchenvy.com, which shows you a ton of slides that early stage companies have used. One common trait among these pitches is they all look good. If your PowerPoint or Apple Keynote skills are not great, hire a designer to help. You can find a good one on Fiverr or eLance, or ask around.

I have included a template for a good pitch deck in the book bonuses which you can access at www.startlaunchgrow.com/nevertoolate-bonuses.

INVESTORS ARE NOT "SHARKS"

If you're like millions of Americans with an interest in entrepreneurship, you probably watch the reality TV show *Shark Tank*. While the show provides insights into the many small business ideas Americans hatch, it doesn't quite represent the real world of raising money from outside investors.

First of all, you almost never convince an investor in a matter of minutes. As we highlighted earlier in the chapter, fundraising is a form of relationship-building that normally happens over weeks or months.

Second of all, it's rare that you will present to multiple competing investors at the same time. It does happen sometimes at showcases or at incubator "demo days," but what almost never happens is a scenario where investors compete with each other in your presence in real time. You would be lucky if you had multiple investors interested, but they will express their interest in the form of a term sheet. If you've received more than one term sheet, by all means you should negotiate to get the best deal.

Third of all, the valuation that the Sharks give is usually based on the revenue and profit that the business is producing *at that time*. In my experience, investors are much more focused on projections and the entrepreneur's plans for achieving them than on current financials.

GET A GREAT LAWYER

When I was a VC, the single biggest factor in getting venture capital financings closed was the quality of company counsel. Experienced counsel knows how to deliver the legal background materials that are part of every VC's due diligence. They know how to draft financing documents in standard terms and how to explain them to entrepreneurs. They know that their job is to get the deal done within reasonable bounds. They protect their client without getting in the way.

Finding great legal counsel is a matter of asking around and doing your research. Many law firms will say they do "corporate and securities" law and they are probably accurate in that description. However, securities law work for a public company is totally different than startup financing.

Look at the firm's website, ask the partners which *early stage* companies they represented for seed or Series A financing, and check references. Also, ask other CEOs and founders what law firms and partners they use and what their experience is with those firms and partners.

One reason you want a firm that really does early stage financings is that they know the current state of the market. They will know what a reasonable valuation is since they and their partners see lots of venture and angel deals.

Another reason you want a law firm that focuses on early stage companies is cost. Law firms that focus on young companies know they can't charge the same hourly rate as when they work with large companies. Most will usually make a special accommodation, either a discounted rate or a flat fee (with limits). They may also defer a portion of their fees until you raise a larger amount of capital and can afford to pay them.

One way to check out a law firm and also to get some free education is to ask the partner you are considering to walk you through the normal terms that you should expect in your term sheet.

Finally, many law firms and investors now use standardized documents in order to keep legal fees to a minimum. There are two or three pretty good legal templates for early stage financings that are widely used. Ask both your law firm and your prospective investors if they will use them. If not, you should ask why not.

The template documents I recommend can be found at www. seriesseed.com and www.techstars.com/docs.

TYPES OF FINANCIAL INSTRUMENTS

There are three basic types of financial instruments used to fund startups: equity, debt, and convertible notes. They each have positives and negatives depending on your investors and the state of development of your company.

EQUITY

For startups, the most common form of security or financial instrument is equity. Selling equity to an investor, whether a friend, family member, or professional investor, means giving them a piece of ownership in your business. You're taking on a partner for life, so don't take it lightly.

There are two main types of equity used in startups: common equity and preferred equity.

Common equity means that the investor is getting the same type of security and the same type of rights you hold as a founder. If you grant new employees equity it will also be common equity. Preferred equity or "stock" means that a shareholder will have preferences that are more advantageous than with common equity.

There are dozens of preferences that investors often include when they purchase preferred equity. The most common include: Liquidation Preference, Board Seats, Information Rights, Pro-rata Rights (the right to participate in future financings), Co-sale rights (a right to sell alongside other sellers), Anti-dilution rights (an adjustment to the purchase price if stock is sold at lower prices), and Right of First Refusal (to buy stock that others may want to sell).

Brad Feld did an excellent series of blog posts explaining all of these which you can find at http://www.feld.com/archives/2005/08/term-sheet-series-wrap-up.html.

DEBT

Selling debt means the investor is loaning you money that you'll have to pay back with interest in a specified period of time. Because your business probably doesn't generate profit or cash flow yet, debt is not a very commonly used security in funding early stage companies. But it does happen sometimes. If you can get the investors to waive your need to pay interest right away, debt can be a great way to fund the business because you are not giving up ownership to the investor.

CONVERTIBLE NOTES

These are basically a hybrid of debt and equity. Issuing a convertible note to an investor is basically giving them debt that will automatically convert into equity when you do a larger fundraising round. The reason to use a convertible note is that it doesn't set a valuation price on the company when you issue it. So you don't get into lengthy debates with investors about how much the company is worth right now. You defer that debate until you either bring in more sophisticated investors or until the business is further along and easier to value.

Investors who take convertible notes will want their note to convert into equity at a discount to the valuation when it gets set. They will also want to set a cap, or maximum price, that their equity will convert.

For example, if you raise $500,000 in a convertible note, the terms of the note are 6 percent interest, 20 percent discount, $6 million valuation cap. When you raise this money, the investors in your note do not own any equity in your company—yet.

A year later, you raise $1.5 million at a $3 million valuation. Your $500,000 note will convert to $600,000 of equity in the new round, because 20 percent of $500,000 is $100,000 additional money that you owe the note holders. You also owe them $30,000 of interest ($500,000 × 6 percent).

If, by chance, you'd been able to raise your $1.5 million at a value higher than $6 million, then you would have to issue shares to the note holders *at* a $6 million valuation, because that was the cap that was set.

NON-TRADITIONAL WAYS TO FUND YOUR BUSINESS

Another way entrepreneurs can fund their companies is to get their customers to do it. Sometimes you can get customers to pay to build a solution. This is called "customer-funded development."

A more common scenario, especially in subscription businesses, is to get the entire subscription payment upfront. This is a huge difference in your cash flow compared to getting paid monthly or quarterly. The challenge with subscription businesses in which you get paid over time is that your expenses for product development and sales commissions are usually paid upfront, creating cash flow challenges.

YOUR FUNDING CHECKLIST

- Have you done a business plan or Lean Canvas?
- Have you validated customer demand and acquisition cost?
- Can your team execute?
- What will make this a big company?
- Why are you the right person to lead the venture?
- Why is now the right time for the company? Why is it the right time for you?

ARE YOU COMMITTED?

The single biggest challenge any mid-life entrepreneur is going to have in raising outside capital is convincing the investor that he's truly committed.

Someone who has lived in a corporate job for twenty years has developed a pattern. You're comfortable. So why are you stepping outside that comfort zone? Why now? Why are you the person to drive this business to success?

As Sara Schaer of KangaDo pointed out, there is no greater equalizer than revenue and customers. In the startup world, it's known as traction, and it makes investors overcome all kinds of other objections.

The bottom line is: go out and kick ass and investors will fall in line if you need them.

YOUR OWN DUE DILIGENCE

As you prepare to fundraise and as you go through the process, you'll want to research investors with as much detail as they will research you. You need to do your "due diligence" both on the firm and its individual partners.

Questions you should consider:

- What are their goals?
- How big is their fund? Is it big enough or too big for you?
- What is their preferred ownership stake?
- What is their ideal stage?

- Do they take a seat on the board of directors? How do they operate as a board member?
- How do they take bad news?
- What kind of assistance do they give their portfolio companies in terms of recruiting and helping to open doors in sales or strategy?
- As the company grows, do they try to build teams around founding CEOs or replace the CEO with someone more experienced?

It is critically important to have a good fit among founders and investors. If the fit between entrepreneur and investor isn't good, it can lead to significant fractures.

Dan Malven, founder and CEO of Analyte Health, went through this kind of issue. When he founded his business, he thought he would have a business that generated a fair amount of cash but had a relatively small market opportunity. As the business grew, he identified factors that changed the business plan. He also saw a much larger opportunity:

> We had to take on the burden of regulatory footprint that we didn't anticipate having. As an entrepreneur, I made those changes mentally pretty fast. And I'm like, "Okay, this is the new world order." Problem was, my investors, they didn't make that turn with me. They were like, "What is the problem here? You sold me on this...growing at X percent per month and here were your contribution margins and where the hell is profitability?"

> My response was, "Well, the market is different than what we thought. This is the new world order we are in and, frankly, it's a much better business. It's a much bigger opportunity than

originally we talked about." They didn't make the turn [with me]. The reason I think they didn't make the turn was because they were small funds. They were small funds whose whole business model was to [come] in at under a $10 million value, and to exit at between $50 [million] and $100 million.

And they couldn't either psychologically or fund-wise bear the risk to invest, [to stay in longer with high-growth], and to look at exiting at $250 million and up.

For Malven, the differences of opinion with his investors and board ultimately led to him leaving the business. So understand how important due diligence is. Bringing on outside investors is like marriage.

YOUR FUNDRAISING MINDSET

You need to prepare yourself to fundraise. It's a long, overly time-consuming process with a huge number of "no" responses. It is like a sales process in many ways, but more difficult. It's more difficult because it's harder to qualify investors than sales prospects.

Unlike in sales, investors will waste your time by taking a meeting even if they're not going to invest. They may be in research mode, trying to learn about sector. They may be eyeing making an investment in a competitor, so they take a meeting with you. They may have little to no money left in their fund, but they take the meeting in order to "look active" in the market. It really doesn't matter why, but you will be in many investor meetings that are a waste of your time.

Think of it as practice. The more times you give your pitch, the better you'll give it. The more times you answer questions, the better you'll get.

Unlike in sales, it only takes one investor to say yes to get a big return.

Remember that funding is a catalyst for your business to grow, not a goal itself. Your goal is to build a great company.

LEGAL ISSUES FOR MID-LIFE FOUNDERS

"Anyone who stops learning is old,
whether at twenty or eighty."

HENRY FORD

WHY LEGAL MATTERS MATTER

Setting up your company and managing the various legal issues is a lot like trying to live a healthy lifestyle. You can ignore your doctor's advice to eat well, get sleep, and exercise and you'll keep on living, for a while. But eventually those choices will catch up with you.

Your startup's legal health is very similar. You can shortchange it at first, but eventually it will catch up with you. You could be sued. You could owe the government in fines or taxes. You could even lose control of the business or the core idea to former employers or other founders.

I understand the reasons why many entrepreneurs short-change their attention on legal matters. They don't really understand what they need to do, it can be confusing, and they fear that getting professional advice is incredibly expensive. After all, law firms are expensive, often charging hundreds of dollars an hour.

But you can and should educate yourself for free. You can also find law firms willing to give you discounts or defer their legal fees in the earliest stages. So take the time to learn what you need to learn now and avoid the huge headaches down the line.

Disclaimer: The author is not a lawyer and neither this chapter nor this book, nor any materials associated with it, give legal advice. None of the lawyers interviewed for the book are giving legal advice through their interviews. You should consult with a lawyer regarding any legal matters relating to your current employment or your new company.

REGARDING YOUR FORMER EMPLOYER...

When you accepted your current or most recent job, you probably agreed to a few things with your employer. You may have signed a non-compete agreement (depending on the state or country you work in). You probably agreed to assign all of your inventions to the company, to not solicit employees or customers after you leave, and to give your full time and effort to the company.

You probably also agreed to use company assets like equipment, software, and Wi-Fi only for the good of the company.

These agreements can affect your new company or your side gig. So you should pull out the company documents you signed and thoroughly read what they say about these issues. You should also consult with your attorney to stay on the right side of the law.

NON-COMPETE

A non-compete agreement is basically what it sounds like. It says that you won't compete with your current employer for a period of time after you leave. You probably signed one (unless you live in California where they are not enforceable) when you started with your current or most recent employer.

Have you pulled out and read through the company documents? Some are worded very strictly, others are looser. Take a look at the "tail" or period of time during which you're prohibited from competition. The most common tail is a year, but it could be longer or shorter.

The other thing to check is the definition of "competition." It could be tightly defined to a niche of a particular industry, such as "supply chain software," or it could be much broader. "Business software" would be hard to enforce, but nevertheless you agreed to it. Or it could leave the definition vague, saying that you agree not to compete in whatever business the company is in.

Even if your startup isn't competing at all with your current company, be sure to carefully read through the legal docs you signed. You'll be referring to them in the sections below.

NON-SOLICITATION

A non-solicitation agreement generally covers two very important prohibitions related to your current or last employer.

The first prohibition is that you agree not to solicit employees. So if you start your company and then start hiring your former colleagues, you will be in violation of the agreement.

These agreements are often difficult to interpret and enforce because of the possibility that employees *approach you* for employment rather than *you solicit them*. Because of this, you can often get away with hiring one or two former colleagues, but don't get into the habit of it. You might get a sternly worded "cease and desist" letter from the old employer's legal team. You could even get sued for violating your agreement.

The other prohibition is closely related to the non-compete section. This part prohibits you from soliciting the company's clients, partners, or consultants. The most heavily enforced part of this relates to the company's clients. If you start trying to take business away from your former employer and you have agreed not to, they are likely to come after you legally. So you really need to know what you can and cannot do, and for how long.

INTELLECTUAL PROPERTY

As a startup founder, "intellectual property" refers to all the ideas and work products you create in your new business.

The formal definition from Wikipedia:

> Intellectual property (IP) is a term referring to creations of the intellect for which a monopoly is assigned to designated owners by law. Some common types of intellectual property rights (IPR) are copyright, patents, and industrial design rights; and the rights that protect trademarks, trade dress, and in some jurisdictions trade secrets: all these cover music, literature, and other artistic works; discoveries and inventions; and words, phrases, symbols, and designs.

Your employment agreement with your current company probably says that anything you do or create using company equipment, technology, Internet connections, or software (basically the stuff they own) belongs to them.

So beware: *if you've used company equipment for your side business, your startup's work may belong to your employer.*

It is absolutely crucial that you check your employment agreement to see what it says about this.

You may also have a problem if you use your own equipment but during your employer's company hours.

If you violate these agreements, your employer could have a claim on your intellectual property. You might think, "Well, that's no big deal. I don't have any patents or anything." But you'd be wrong. The claims could include your work product, such as software code, logos, copyrights, or other forms of intellectual property.

Since you don't have the time or money to face this kind of lawsuit, take the care needed to work on your new company *outside* of normal working hours and on your own personal computer. Don't take startup calls during work time. Be cognizant of your risks and you should be fine.

YOUR FOUNDERS' AGREEMENT

A "founders' agreement" is a legal document that outlines the division of equity between/among the founders and the conditions of that equity. Thoughtfully setting up a founders' agreement is one of the most important activities you can undertake for your young company. Getting this wrong can have disastrous consequences. Disputes and lawsuits are common in founder separations, especially when there are no founders' agreements.

One of the most important provisions of the agreement is that the ownership of the founders' equity must vest over time, or be "earned." This means that if one party walks away, they don't continue to earn their equity.

Vesting periods and schedules can vary, but the most common vesting is over four years. This means that each founder "earns" a little piece of his or her equity every month for four years. I have also seen schedules where the equity is vested in quarterly increments, which means it is earned every three months.

Here is an example: your startup has two founders, you and another founder. You decide to split the equity 50/50 to each party (not always the best idea, but we'll cover that later). You agree that the equity should vest monthly over four years. One year in, your cofounder leaves the business to go earn a larger and steadier paycheck. Instead of walking away with half the company, your cofounder gets 25 percent of 50 percent, or 12.5 percent, of the founders' stock. He gets 25 percent because he worked for one year (out of the four that he needed to earn all of his founders' stock). You end up with 87.5 percent of the founders' stock rather than 50 percent, which makes sense because you are continuing to work on the business and he has left the business.

To some people, this makes all the sense in the world. To others, it seems unfair. Some argue, "Why do I need to *earn* my equity? I'm taking a huge risk to start the company." Others argue that it's unnecessary: "I know my cofounder. We've been coworkers for years. He would never leave the business."

There are literally dozens of very good reasons that a cofounder leaves a startup. Sometimes the startup changes direction to something the cofounder isn't passionate about. Sometimes the cofounders argue and can't get along. Sometimes a life circumstance like divorce, a health issue, a death in the family, or a kid's drug problem causes the founder to leave. The bottom line is you cannot predict those circumstances. A founders' agreement protects the founders who will continue to work in the new business.

There is one last reason to have an agreement with vesting: investors will generally demand one, so you might as well have one in place. Investors don't want to see a founder walk away with a lot of equity if they are no longer working in the business. They know that only the working team is dedicated to making a return for the investor. They want everyone to be motivated to build as big a business as possible for all investors and employees.

There are a few nuances of founders' agreements that you'll want to think about and have your attorneys craft to your liking. One relates to how the vesting works if a founder gets fired. Any founder, including the CEO, could perform poorly and may need to be replaced. Sometimes this is amenable to all involved, but more often it's pretty contentious. If a founder has a vesting schedule for his/her equity, it's always possible they could get fired and not earn very much of their total equity.

You can address that possibility upfront in the agreement or you can choose to deal with it at a later time. One possible solution is to offer "partial vesting acceleration" to a fired founder. This means that the company would accelerate the vesting of the founder's equity so that they walk away with more than they had earned, but not all of it. The possibility of a founder being fired increases significantly when you take on external investors and board members. Investors and management don't always see eye-to-eye on major issues.

The other important nuance you might want to deal with in the founders' agreement is the possibility that the new business is acquired before the vesting period is completed. This is called a "change of control" and is triggered by the company selling a controlling interest, more than 51 percent, to another party. You could choose to vest all of the founders' equity, which is called "full vesting acceleration." You could vest some of the founders' unvested equity, called "partial acceleration." Or you could choose not to vest any of the unvested equity. Lastly, you can choose to vest the founders' equity only after an acquisition *and* a second event, such as the founder being fired by the acquiring company. This is called a "double trigger" since it requires both events to occur before the vesting acceleration.

There is no right answer when it comes to this decision. The most founder-friendly way is full acceleration on change of control. After all, the founders have delivered a return to the investors in the form of an acquisition—why shouldn't they get a payday as well?

The investors will argue that an acquiring company wants the management team and employees to stick around and help build the combined business. If the founders all get full acceleration, then they can walk away rather than stay with the acquiring company. The investor point is that acquiring companies will adjust the price they pay downward if they know there is a risk the founders will leave.

Usually a partial acceleration or a double-trigger is a reasonable compromise. Of course, you may not want to deal with this until you take on investors. But be aware that most sophisticated investors will insist on founder vesting, and remember that change-of-control provisions for vesting are one of the most common issues for negotiation.

WHY TO INCORPORATE

At some point you're going to want to incorporate your new company. Incorporation is the legal process of forming the new corporation, choosing the name and state in which you will set up the business, the classes of stock, and the directors and officers. The process varies depending on your state.

Incorporating is a very important process for a mid-life entrepreneur because the act of incorporating will protect most of your personal assets in the event of a lawsuit against the company. There are some situations in which your personal assets might be at risk.

If you're in the idea-testing phase of starting your new business, you probably don't need to incorporate just yet. The company doesn't really have any assets and the operations are so limited that the risk of a lawsuit is very low.

As you start hiring employees or contractors and begin generating intellectual property like software code, websites, blog posts, product descriptions, and the like, you'll want to incorporate. You have some legal and tax choices to make when you get ready to incorporate, such as Limited Liability Company (LLC), C Corp, or S Corp (taxed at the individual rather than corporate level).

There is a cost associated with incorporating (and often with winding down a company), so you want to think through the right timing. It's easy to wait too long, which will open you up to personal risk of losing your assets.

CLASSES OF STOCK

Generally speaking, you don't need to set up different classes of stock until you start raising outside capital for your new company. I'm covering this here as basic education, but your business attorney can do a better job, so be sure to ask them.

Most founders receive common stock in the company. Even though I've referred to it as "founders' stock," it is just common stock or common equity. When you raise outside capital, you can issue either more common stock or, more likely, preferred stock or equity. Most investors will insist on preferred stock because it has additional "preferences" over common, hence the name.

Normally, receiving something from a business is a taxable event, so your common stock should be considered income for tax purposes. However, since your business is brand new and really doesn't have any value, there should be almost no tax due.

Again, please consult with your company's attorney and with your personal tax professional.

STOCK OPTIONS

Other than the founders' common stock, most of the equity you will issue for new employees, advisors, consultants, and board of directors' members will be in the form of stock options. You will likely establish a "pool" of options so that you can make those grants out of the pool.

You have probably received a few grants of options or restricted stock from a previous employer. The way it works is that the company issues the stock option to the employee (or advisor) and the employee has the right to actually purchase the stock at some point in the future at a certain price, called the "strike price" or "exercise price."

Options almost always have some kind of vesting schedule, and you can vary that depending on the circumstance. For employees, the most common is a four-year vesting schedule with a one-year "cliff." The cliff means that the employee won't vest any stock until the one-year anniversary of their start at the company. This is to avoid a bad hire walking away with equity. If you know someone is a poor fit, and you need to terminate them after a few months, you would hate to have them as a shareholder in your company. After the one-year cliff, most grants are vested ratably for the next three years, either monthly or quarterly.

Here is an example: let's say you grant a key employee 1,000 stock options with four-year vesting and a one-year cliff. On the one-year anniversary of his option grant, he vests 250 options. (He still doesn't own the stock. He has to *exercise* his option for that.) He still has 750 options that will vest monthly, and thirty six months remaining (one year for the first chunk, plus thirty six months equals four years). Every month after the one-year anniversary, he vests 20.833 additional options (1/36 × 750). If he leaves or is fired before the four years is up, he can only exercise his vested options.

Besides being a founder, being an early employee in a startup can be a very lucrative way of generating wealth because of stock options. The possibility of significant wealth generation is what will attract most of your early employees and advisors.

You're going to want to develop a rough plan of how much equity you plan to grant your employees over the next twelve months. This is to be sure that your pool is large enough, and to be sure that you are in the ballpark in terms of these equity grants.

You should expect to have to grant more equity to a more critical or more senior new hire. You should also expect that the equity for those people will go down as you raise money, achieve profitability, get your product selling, or otherwise reduce the risk for the new employee. Think of options like this: they compensate your new hires for the risk of joining a new business with as much uncertainty as yours has.

There are no hard and fast rules for how much equity your employees should get at each stage. It depends on your type of business, on the competition for talent in your region, and on the stage of development of the company. You should ask your advisors and mentors to help guide your thinking. Attorneys often have a good gauge, as do current CEOs and heads of HR. Sometimes CFOs will have a good feel as well, since they often manage the overall capitalization of the company.

For a high-tech startup, the expected equity that a new employee would receive at the various funding stages might look something like this:

OPTIONS PERCENTAGE BY COMPANY STAGE

Role	Seed	Series A	Series B
Vice President	2.5-4.0%	1.5-2.5%	1.0%
Director	1.0-2.0%	.75-1.25%	.25-.75%
Manager/Senior Contributor	.75-1.5%	.25-.75%	.10-.25%
Individual Contributor	.25-.50%	.1-.25%	.05-.1%

(Before I start receiving e-mails or tweets about how wrong the table is, it is only meant to be illustrative and general. Numbers may be different in your region or industry.)

As you start to plan your hiring and build your option pool, you will want to plan out one year to eighteen months' worth of option grants in order to build the pool properly. The reason is that investors like to know how much of the company they will own *after* the options are issued. Going back to your investors to get more options put into the pool is a bit of a pain because it is the investors' share to be reduced, or diluted.

KEEPING RECORDS AND KEEPING IT LEGAL

You will want to keep track of every shareholder in the company, the type of stock they have, the date they received it, and the provisions of their grant, including the vesting schedule and the price. You can do this with a spreadsheet at first. This is called a capitalization table, or "cap table" in startup lingo.

Record keeping is critically important for a business, especially in regards to equity. There are a multitude of reasons for this, not the least of which is the IRS.

There are a number of items you'll want to make sure you have in place before you start raising money for your new startup. These are:

- Your incorporation documents.
- Your capitalization table and details.
- Any debt that the business has incurred.
- Any major agreements that could impact the company.

Getting yourself a good attorney who understands startups and the legal and business issues you are facing is a key step for most successful founders. A great attorney can be one of your most trusted advisors.

John Gilluly is managing partner and executive committee member of the Texas offices of DLA Piper, one of the largest law firms in the world. He has advised me on numerous venture capital and startup opportunities, and had this to say about how mid-life entrepreneurs deal with equity and risk containment:

> I would say generally that older entrepreneurs are typically more sensitive or aware of the risks of putting everything at stake

and going out and starting a new venture, [probably] because of experience and vintage or the demands of life and families and children.

And so, what I often see with older entrepreneurs is the transition from a current employment, where they're getting a regular paycheck and benefits, to the new venture that is slower than the twenty-something [who] really doesn't have anything to lose.

What I see with older entrepreneurs is they will work on the new business while they continue to work [a day job]. And once it starts to...take shape, and in particular once they are actually at a point where they may raise capital, you'll see them transition [full time to the startup]... It is much more frequent to find an older entrepreneur...controlling their risk.

Whether or not it's a single person or whether there is a group of them, that's really driven as much by the nature of the idea as it is by anything else. If it's hard science and it's a professor... or an engineer who has developed this idea...that's often a solo start and...they will quickly find a business person or facilitator to help them...or have junior engineers or scientists to help them. If it's a software or Internet idea or an app, that can be a team sometimes.

When I'm dealing with older entrepreneurs, I generally find them—I wouldn't say risk-averse, but I would say risk-aware... and more careful about the transition from working within a company...to the new venture.

It's not unprecedented that somebody does just go for it and jumps off the cliff, but it definitely is the exception to the rule... They'll work nights and weekends on their idea off the clock until it takes shape and they have confidence that there's something there, whether financeable or in the market with the product or whatever it may be. That's generally the way that they work.

For instance, from my perspective, we're often dealing with existing employer arrangements...what the current employer's rights are in respect to intellectual property...and make sure we are delineating between activities done while at work or on work equipment versus independently on their own, trying not to comingle ideas and energy between the two ventures.

With [younger entrepreneurs]...you'll have four of them living in an apartment and they're waiting tables or whatever they're doing to get by, or their parents may be paying rent, or whatever... and they kind of don't care, they don't have anything to lose... no responsibilities...all they have to do is have a roof over their head and food on the plate.

One of the first items on the table when we meet with a founder team is making it real for them that the almost inevitable outcome [is] that one or more of the people are going to leave. I'm not saying they would leave because they're a bad person, but it just happens in life. And they may become disenfranchised maybe for valid reason, or they have a financial difficulty and they have to go back and get a job...or they can get divorced or whatever.

Your life becomes more complex and things happen, so what we always do is...work very early on and very diligently at making sure that we delineate who gets the equity if people leave, what the rights are if there are certain major life events for one of the major founders...so that when the inevitable happens, we're not stuck trying to figure it out after the fact.

We often have [these kinds of founder issues]. I've got one right now. There were two founders, one of them left, they split the equity 50/50, there was no vesting, there was no personal agreement or stock agreement or anything like that, and one of them decided he didn't want to do it anymore.

We've had all types of different mediations to deal with those situations... Sometimes the founders can work it out themselves. I've sat down with clergy and the founders and handled it that way. There have been all different types of solutions to the issue, and sometimes it doesn't work out and [the startup] dies. That's unfortunate, but that's reality. When we sit down with them, one of the first things we talk about, absolutely, is founder agreements.

It's...a process of getting them to appreciate the formalities of running a business. Older entrepreneurs respect and appreciate this more than the younger entrepreneurs do. It's a process, right? It's organizing the business, issuing the equity, having the types of rights and restrictions around the equity...basic agreements and NDAs [author's note: NDAs are "non-disclosure agreements"] and so forth. Not promising people equity based on the fly, or even implicitly promising them some type of return for their contributing intellectual capital to their venture.

People that have been in business for a long time and have been in environments where there is rigor and structure around the formalities of a business are much more conscientious of that, just because they've got the experience and [have] seen what happens when you're not formal about it. And so you know, getting them to appreciate that, getting them to recognize the consequence of not doing that, is paramount.

Older, more experienced founders know what they're good at. They are more aware of what they're good at and what they're not. They're not burdened as much with trying to figure out who they are.

I mean they come into a situation and they know what their skills are, they know what their background gives them, brings to the table, and gives them perspective on, and they know where they need help, whether internally or externally.

With the junior [founders], we spend a lot of time saying, "Hey, look, your business may be different, but we generally see people do [certain types of common things], in terms of internal staffing or hiring or transitioning from outside advisors like a CFO or whatever the particular situation requires."

[Older entrepreneurs]...have a network, and they are much more comfortable...with experienced directors. The boards are typically constituted very differently than the junior entrepreneur boards. The junior entrepreneur boards...often will just be the local tech players. Like, it could be somebody from, let's say Austin, it could be somebody who is a local, the guy with The Capital Factory or Tech Ranch or somebody who's [a] well-known, local tech guy plus the money guys.

The more senior, experienced entrepreneur may have a person like that on the board, but they are looking for a much different profile. They are looking for somebody [who] has a deeper experience set, brings different things to the table. Those boards are just very different.

There's nothing better in my experience than having people in the boardroom who have been around the block a bunch of times and can give guidance to management.

I see differences in terms of management of the board. Being able to manage the board, communicate effectively to the board, knowing what the board needs to know and doesn't, and what level of detail, information shared with the board.

But in terms of helping the board succeed in its role, as the ultimate oversight body, as well as to try to provide value based on experience, I find older entrepreneurs are much more effective at that, just because they've worked longer, they likely had that experience in the past...they know what's relevant and what's not relevant. They know the level of detail that's necessary as opposed to the alternative. So it's just a much more mature process.

No one puts it better or understands risk containment better than Gilluly, which is why I value his counsel. So do as I both say and do. You'll need a good business attorney so be sure you have one in your network.

FAMILY & STARTUP LIFE

---

*"A man should never neglect
his family for business."*

WALT DISNEY

Personal circumstances play a large role in the timing of
becoming a founder. One of the most important of these is
family. The hours and emotional investment of founding a
startup can put significant stress on a marriage and on your
ability to parent.

Most mid-career founders in their late thirties or forties have
a spouse and children, and it is fair to say that family considerations, particularly having and raising young children, can
be one of the most significant timing considerations.

Many prospective founders with very young children decide
to wait until their children are somewhat older, or much older,

before starting a company. As anyone who has raised infants knows, it's a sleep deprived, stressful couple of years. If you go through it a few times, as our family has been blessed to do, you know that the challenges and stress can compound. Starting a company in the middle of raising infants could be a huge challenge for the founder, the family, and the company.

However, it doesn't necessarily get easier to start a company when the kids become of school age. Yes, you're probably getting more sleep, but now you're shuttling kids to afterschool and weekend activities.

Sara Schaer, founder of the mobile app KangaDo, which helps parents manage their daily transportation challenges with children, experienced these issues:

> While the kids were little, I experienced all kinds of permutations of work schedules. It was pretty brutal. I had a partner who was not really available physically or work-schedule-wise to shoulder the brunt of the child care. I was unwilling to completely "outsource"...[the kids] 24/7 to someone else.
>
> [Doing a startup]...just wouldn't have been the right fit for me then. Plus, I came to be aware of this particular problem as they got older. I feel like I am not out of the woods yet, I still have this problem, but I have a lot of hindsight to what people need and when. And at the same time, schedule-wise, and resource-wise, it would not have been possible to replace myself with full time child care.

ARE STARTUPS COMPATIBLE WITH FAMILY?

The popular press likes to push the idea that startup founders work around the clock, and that startups are not compatible with family. Many of us have read stories about startup founders sleeping in the office under their desk, working eighty-hour weeks or more. Early Facebook employees with children were encouraged to have their kids come by the office, so they could say goodnight.

The stresses that startups put on marriage can take a huge toll. A recent *Inc.* magazine article highlighted a number of high-profile divorces among successful entrepreneurs, including Sergey Brin of Google and Penelope Trunk of Brazen Careerist. The article likened starting a company to having an affair. The passion of the entrepreneur gets poured into the company and thus the marriage and family suffer.[34] It's like there's a third partner in the marriage.

So what does that mean for your startup dreams if you're in your thirties, forties, or fifties and you have a family? Does it mean you should wait to start a company? Or wait until you're rich enough to hire a nanny? Or wait until your spouse can stay home with the kids?

I don't think it means any of those things. However, you should be clear that there are some tradeoffs you're going to face.

For Kelly Cooper, founder and chief merchandising officer of QOR, there were challenges and tradeoffs:

I'm lucky because I have a husband who takes the lead in caring for our two daughters and frankly for me...he's super supportive. He's a private chef. He doesn't have a day job, if you will. He usually works on the weekends when I'm not working, or at least not at the office. So that honestly really helps. But I would say since I've been involved in QOR, I just feel like I've screwed up a lot more. I am over-scheduled.

For instance, I had a breakfast appointment yesterday for a non-profit, and I completely missed it. I have a lot of balls in the air so, naturally, I feel like I've disconnected from parts of my life. I guess I've lost track of some of my friends through this last year. I feel especially adrift with my girlfriends. They are really important to me, so I would say that has been a casualty of my startup mode. And some of my hobbies have fallen to the wayside, although I make time for exercise. As for my family, I have been able to be present for them, so I don't feel like my family has suffered.

Your personal drive is another factor in play. Those of us crazy enough to start companies tend to really pour ourselves into things. We care. We obsess. We identify ourselves with the business in a huge way. We are slightly crazy and we cannot stomach the idea of failure, so we let the business subsume our friendships and relationships.

I think founders do tend to work more than people in corporate jobs, but to some degree it's because they want to. Founders take huge pride in ownership and the success of their business. They feel a certain amount of desperation to succeed, the tug of too much to do and limited staff to do it. It seems as though there is always more work to be done.

However, I don't think it has to be this way. Older entrepreneurs with families can and do start companies while also finding quality time for loving, supportive relationships with their families. One's spouse and kids can be a crucial and important balance to the entrepreneurial life. Playing Legos for thirty minutes with your kids can be the time away from the business that you need. And yes, you do need time away from your business.

You need time to think, to breathe, to love, to exercise, and to recharge your body and brain. Don't think of it as "time not spent on your business," but essential elements to making your company more successful.

While there are tradeoffs, they don't have to be complete and total. Your family relationships can add to the business. According to Sam Altman, CEO of Silicon Valley incubator Y Combinator: "You can have a startup and one other thing. You can have a family, but you probably can't have many other hobbies."

So how can you make it work?

COMMUNICATING WITH YOUR FAMILY

Almost all of the entrepreneurs I spoke with had huge support from their spouse. This is crucial. The emotional ups and downs of startups are tough to weather if the relationship with your spouse is rocky.

The first step is making sure your spouse understands what you are getting into and why. Have you explained what you expect the tradeoffs will be? What about the hours and the stress you expect to bear?

On the flip side, have you shared your motivations? If your spouse sees and understands your motivations, not only will they understand why you're going to start the business, they can also help to remind you of those motivations when your spirits are down.

What about your kids? Have you let them know that you are starting a new business and that you might be less available to them? My kids were somewhat older when I started my company, and they thought it was *so cool* that I was starting and running a business. They also really liked hearing about the high-level concepts of getting a website running, marketing concepts like split testing landing pages and marketing copy, and content marketing.

Starting a business is very stressful and requires long hours and huge commitment, but it's more than that. Many other careers demand long hours and commitment. Startups pack a double whammy. The entrepreneur is also putting his family's financial situation at risk.

Ongoing communication with your family is even more important than upfront communication. Make sure everyone understands the reasons you're working late, traveling, or frequently on the phone putting out fires. They might even offer you new perspectives in making critical decisions.

Make "checking in" with your family a priority. They will want to know how the business is doing, and you'll want to know about their daily life, schoolwork, sports teams, and other activities.

John Levisay, founder of Craftsy, has a good perspective on balancing startups and family:

> All of us [founders] had young children, with the exception of one. It forces focus in that you can't be sitting around the office until two or three in the morning on a consistent basis. Oftentimes, [with] young founders, there is a lot of socializing, almost sandbagging of focus, because you know you are going to be at the office until midnight.

> I think I had been lucky in that I think my spouse believed in me and fully understood the gravity of the undertaking. I have seen people fail because there was not a real understanding...it's like, "Why aren't you home? Why are you on the phone? What are you doing?"

> And it begins to weigh on people if their spouse is not—and this is female or male, either gender—[someone who] understands the gravity and the risk of this undertaking...and the stress that goes along with it... What is the upside and what is the eventual plan? Because I think if there's not a light at the end of the tunnel, like anything, it can become...you know, if my wife thought this was going to be how life was for the next twenty or thirty years, it would be very problematic.

> And so, we had very honest discussions about time periods of

what this would involve, and sacrifices we would have to make, personally...we have two young kids...and professionally, there was risk...there was a good chance it wasn't going to work. She was just on board and that's how she continues to be and that's really helped.

I understand that my family, my wife and kids, are very important, and they still are going to be there even if this fails. I guess [I] just keep perspective and realize that if I come home for dinner, that during those two and a half hours, to have the discipline to say, "If I get to this at 9:30 tonight when everyone's in bed, nothing is going to change. Nothing is happening between now and tomorrow morning...that I can't address between ten and twelve at night.

So being able to compartmentalize and be present when you're home. There are a lot of people that are home a lot but they're never really there. They're constantly checking e-mail, they're zoning out in front of the TV, they aren't listening to their children or wife. So having discipline around the time you are home, being present, I think it mitigates stress at home and it's fulfilling.

FAMILY PRIORITIES

It might seem self-evident, but if your family is a priority in your life, then you have to act like it. You and your family will need to decide which family events matter the most. Some founders carve out specific nights when they make every effort to get home for dinner. They don't schedule business dinners, networking events, or allow themselves to work late on those nights.

Other founders make it home almost every night. For them, dinnertime and getting the kids to bed is family time. After that they log back in for another couple hours of work. Remember the story of New Relic founder Lew Cirne, who made a point to leave the office every night at 5:00 because dinner with his family is one of the most important things in his life.

For me, the challenge was finding family time combined with the hours of a startup and my commute. We were located in a great accelerator program but it was an hour from our house, so making it home for dinner meant leaving at 5:00 or 6:00. The way I managed it was to have certain days that I would leave for dinner, and certain days I would not. Those expectations were communicated.

Tim Enwall, CEO of Revolv, acquired by Google, has founded multiple companies. As he got older and had a family, he made sure to carve out time for them.

> You know, you're in your thirties or forties, you do have a family and one of the most important pieces of advice I got from an older woman who ran the startup I left when creating my first one... She said, "You know what? I learned very early to maniacally carve out 6:00 to 8:00 as family time and when I didn't do that I had all kinds of work stress and all kinds of family stress, but when I did do that, you know, I was relatively balanced...and my family was relatively okay."

> So, I've done that for sixteen years. My wife is busy, so she's often not available from 6:00 to 8:00, but, by and large, we still try to allocate that time to each other. And, because I'm able to

delegate well, I don't spend twelve [to] fourteen hours a day seven days a week building a business.

FAMILY AS MOTIVATION

For many mid-life entrepreneurs, their family is one of their key motivations. The long hours and extra stress is totally worth it *because* of their family.

For me, seeing my kids in the morning is a huge energy lift and emotional anchor for my life. I probably didn't draw on this as much as I should have when I was in the depths of my startup experiences. I have learned, however, and I do now with my writing and other side projects.

Maybe you dream about getting wealthy so you can leave that wealth to your family. Or perhaps your motivations are subtler. You know that your corporate job and your boss are okay, but they aren't fulfilling your true promise. You want to leave a mark on the world and your family is part of that mark.

I know that is true for me. One of my goals as a parent is to teach my children how to strive, how to plan, how to be self-sufficient, and how to be resilient. I think and hope they see these things in me when they see me working hard on something I care about, like writing a book or building a new business. I am also trying to impart entrepreneurial and technical skills to my kids as I learn them for myself.

It could also be that your motivation in starting a business is to be able to work from home and be with your family more.

Control of your life and interaction with your family is *the* motivation, rather than simply being one of your motivations. I think that's great and I know many bloggers and solo practitioner consultants who do exactly this. If you build your business right, you can have the freedom to work from home, from the beach, or from anywhere.

For Van Barker, founder of YardStash, soccer practice is one of the family events that is most important to him. Since he is running his startup from home, commuting isn't something he needs to worry about, so he can set his schedule to enable himself to coach his kids in soccer.

> I'm the main guy who picks up our two kids at school and takes them to soccer and I cook dinner and so forth. So, I think it's a give and take. I have been very aware that if I can contribute in ways by virtue of being in my situation, and then I work at night a lot. So I think it's trying to be real present when I can with the family, but often knowing that on weekends and nights, I'm going to have to put some hours in.

FAMILY CAN RECHARGE YOU

One of the most important aspects of managing a family together with a startup is to change your mindset about work/life balance. Family activities do not have to be *time away* from your startup. The love, support, motivation, and energy you derive from your family can recharge you and make you a better founder. It can make you more thoughtful, more patient, and help you think more clearly, and it can add to your energy.

Having a family can contribute to your personal success in a number of ways. First, having a spouse and kids can make you motivated to succeed, because failure has a real impact on your financial future. Use that motivation to power through those times when you are down or struggling.

The second way family contributes to your success is energy. I tried to orient my schedule so I could see my kids and wife almost every day. Every morning when I see my kids, I get a good-morning hug, which is a really energizing thing for me. Thank goodness that my oldest child, a teenager, doesn't brush that off just yet.

It is critically important to schedule time with family. Are there some things you won't budge on? Do you really enjoy coaching little league or making sure you're at piano recitals? Setting some real boundaries can help you and your family deal with the energy you are putting into your startup, and even maximize it.

Part of that scheduling process is one-on-one time with your spouse. You need a regular "date night" or time "off the grid" together. Your spouse is probably already concerned about the risk of your startup, so "losing you" to the time demands is doubly hard for them. Making special time for your spouse can help them understand what you're doing and why. They'll see your energy and happiness as a flip side to the stress.

Venture capitalist and former entrepreneur Brad Feld and his wife, Amy, do this regularly:

Every...first of the month we go out to dinner together, something called "life dinner." It doesn't have to be fancy. We give each other a gift, ranging from nice jewelry or a piece of art at one end of the spectrum to one time she gave me a remote-controlled fart machine. Those evenings we reflect on the previous month and look forward to the next month. It's not structured. We've done that for the last ten years.[35]

When it's time for the family, make it your business to be really present with them. I know it's hard to put down the smartphone, but your family knows when your head is buried in your work. The few minutes you think you'll gain is probably a loss, because you lose the time that you could have been with them. You lose the chance to connect emotionally, clear your head, and recharge. It will make you a better parent *and* a better founder.

A recent study in the journal *Pediatrics* by researchers at Boston University Medical Center demonstrated a range of distracted parenting behaviors as parents in a restaurant tapped away on smartphones and were distracted rather than parenting. These behaviors included decreased responsiveness to children, decreased conversation with children, and near constant engagement with the device and not with the children. Many of the kids acted out to get their parents' attention.[36]

It's really tough to be a great founder, parent, or spouse unless you have your own methods and tools for managing your stress. It's important to decompress. Your family and your business will be better for it.

FAMILY BUSINESS

Increasingly, business professionals are not just looking for work/life balance with a separation of their business and personal lives. People are integrating the two in ways that work. There are ways that you, as an older entrepreneur, can incorporate your family into your startup.

One way to integrate your family in the company is to include them. Let your family help in the business or, at a bare minimum, let them see you in the office. Let them see the company you are building. Many successful businesses, once they make it through startup, actually become "family-owned companies."

Can your spouse or kids help out? Does your spouse know accounting or marketing?

Eric Groves, founder of Alignable, includes family whenever possible:

> I do talk to them a lot about the business. My son's really interested in it...[and] my daughter came and worked with me for the summer. And that helps, because they kind of go through it with you. Every time I pick my son up from school, he's like, "Hey, what went on today? What partner did you guys close? How many new businesses?" So, the more that they're a part of what you're doing, the easier it is on everybody I think.

Similarly, Brandi Temple, founder of online clothing company Lolly Wolly Doodle, asked family and friends to pitch in as she was struggling to meet the demands of her growing business.

She filled her garage with friends and family helping as seamstresses. By day, they would sew dresses and boys' rompers, post them on Facebook, and take orders. At night, they would send out invoices and ship product. Everybody pitched in. Her husband, Will, learned to monogram. Her dad would cook a family meal, and everybody would sit around the kitchen working late into the night.[37]

It's pretty normal to feel a push-pull between your new business and your family. Understanding the challenge is half the battle, and you can work with your family on it. Try to make it about work *and* life as opposed to work *slash* life, as if they are totally distinct things. Most of the successful founders I spoke with incorporate parts of their family life into their new business, and bring parts of their work lives home.

Walter Cruttenden, founding CEO of Acorns, a personal investment app that is growing extremely fast, took the concept one step further. He started the company with his son and gave him huge responsibility, making him COO. He plans to turn the business over to him as well.

Cruttenden had founded a number of securities businesses in the past. His son Jeff had the original idea for Acorns based on observations of his friends and peers in college. Acorns was a perfect combination of Walter's deep industry knowledge and years of business experience and Jeff's spark of an idea and passion for this market segment.

TAKE TIME TO ADJUST

You're a passionate, driven, arguably crazy founder who desperately wants his business to be successful. You're a dedicated, loving, family-oriented person who wants to be a good parent and a good spouse. How in the world can you make both of these work?

There is no doubt that work/life balance gets more challenging when you start a company. Startups demand so much time, energy, and emotion that they can seem to swallow you whole.

Try to keep it all in perspective. Your business will still be there if you take an hour a day away for your family. As we have shown, the hour or two a day you give your family might make you more productive and clearer headed as a leader. The company is not life or death, although some days on the startup roller coaster might feel like that. In the beginning, as you are learning to adjust to your new startup, try to go easy on yourself. Do what you can.

On the flip side, your kids are resilient. They will learn a lot from seeing you devote yourself to something passionately.

Ultimately, you will probably be part of more than one startup. Startups can be wildly successful or fail. Your relationships, though, will be with you throughout your life. This perspective can be really valuable when you're desperately trying to fit it all in.

DAILY ROUTINES

There are a number of routines that can help you be more effective as a leader and in your family life.

Try to have a routine with your family. Kids do well with routines—bed times, soccer practice, meal times. It's not that you need to be there for everything; you probably won't be. But it can help everyone if they know you'll be home on certain days and for certain events, daily routines like taking the kids to school, or family dinner.

Have a routine with your spouse. As we showed earlier, relationships between partners get frayed during startups. Having date nights, like Brad Feld, time off the grid, or another form of regular shared time can keep communication flowing for the better.

Startups are chaotic and daily schedules will vary, but routines can help your productivity. Plan your days and establish your priorities first.

If you're working from home or building a lifestyle business, be mindful of having both time and space allocated for work. Carve out a space that is yours, not the kitchen table, so that your family knows where and when you're working, and also when you are available to them.

LEAD BY EXAMPLE

The most important way to make family part of your company culture is to lead by example. Lew Cirne had been part of startups where the culture was all about long hours, so when he founded New Relic, he wanted to operate differently. He had a young child and wanted to be home for dinner every day. It wasn't only about himself; he designed the company so he and his employees could do exactly that: "Certainly I [didn't] want it to be, 'Oh, Lew the founder gets away with it,' [so] it's a pretty quiet office between 5:00 and 5:30 at New Relic compared to most other high-growth companies."

Be mindful of what signals you are sending your team. You can't be asking them to work late if you're not going to. This is part of the company culture that you're going to establish, explored more deeply in Chapter 7.

According to Tim Enwall, CEO of startup Revolv:

> Our founders were in their thirties and forties, too, so they all had homes, they all had families and, frankly, many of the first engineers that tech companies tend to hire tend to be quite experienced engineers. So they often have families. Our culture is very much a culture [where] the office empties out at 6:00, but everybody's working online at 8:00 or 9:00. Everybody's checking in code or debugging or marketing, working online, and we have a corporate culture around chat. So lots of people are chatting in the evenings.

STARTUP + FULL TIME JOB + FAMILY

Making time for your family *and* your startup while working a full time job is especially challenging. The bottom line is that you have three huge priorities. Talk about time pressure!

However, balancing it all can be done—at least for a while. One of the keys I think is to realize that the juggling act will probably end. Either the startup will be successful enough that you can quit your day job, or perhaps hire someone to run it for you, or it will fail and you'll have to start working on another startup idea.

Knowing that something challenging will have an end makes it easier to get through. Your internal monologue is important in helping to manage it: "For this year, it's going to be crazy. But after we hit these milestones, then the business will have enough revenue to support me." Or if you're going after a really high-growth opportunity, maybe the business will have enough traction that you can raise outside capital for salaries and growth requirements.

But while you're in the middle of the crazy balancing act, it requires a mix of really good time management, really good communication with your family, and some sacrifice. Knowing yourself and your productive times can really help.

Writing this book and launching my blog while I had a full time job was very similar to running a startup on the side. I got up weekday mornings at 5:30 to get some time to write and manage the technical aspects of the blog. On weekends I tried to carve out a few hours, especially in the mornings, before our crazy weekend life of errands and kids' activities kicked in.

I planned as much as I could by setting particular times to get particular things done. I brought a notebook to soccer practice to grab an extra half hour of writing time.

The hardest part of working from home is setting good boundaries, both physical and mental. Most lifestyle entrepreneurs I know struggle with this a bit. What hours are you going to work on your business? Do you have a dedicated space for it? Do you have a routine?

Just as important, maybe more important, for lifestyle entrepreneurs, is you need to have a sense of how your business is going to sustain you. Don't underestimate how lonely it can be working from home. Even though coworkers can be a pain in the ass, they do become your friends, and interaction with them is important. Interaction is not as immediate when working from home.

The bottom line is that you can start a business when you have a family. It requires discipline to manage your time and significant communication with your spouse and coworkers. Don't let your perception of the difficulty scare you away from becoming an entrepreneur. Having a supportive, loving family and a thriving new business is worth whatever sacrifices you need to make.

GETTING UNSTUCK

_____

_"Success is not final, failure is not fatal: it
is the courage to continue that counts."_

WINSTON CHURCHILL

In every entrepreneurial venture I have ever seen, there comes
a time when the founder or founders simply feel "stuck." The
business is not making progress and they are not sure where
to turn.

Feeling stuck involves a state of mind. Entrepreneurs create
all kinds of mental traps, excuses, reasons, and barriers. Many
struggle with motivation at times. They procrastinate on things
they know they should be doing. They get distracted by the
Internet or they get lost in a million details while failing to stay
focused on the most important things for the day or week. Think
back to the matrix that Stephen Covey recommends (Chapter
4), with the most important, and most urgent, activities.

Entrepreneurs can lose track of the big picture—their big "*why*." If you connect to your *why*, you can feel *pulled* to get things done, rather than having to *push* yourself.

Your *why* has to be powerful. It has to motivate you to take action when you don't want to, to get off the sofa and spend thirty minutes working on your business when you don't feel like it. Your *why* will help you get up at 5:00 in the morning to write that blog post or to work on your website or to take the next critical action in your plan.

Visualize your *why* regularly. Think about the future state when you are there: when your book is in print or when your product has shipped or when you are running your business from the beach in Spain.

Personally, I use a method adapted from motivational speaker Tony Robbins. I visualize my life the way I want it to be. I do this every morning, and it helps me set up my day so that my activities are the ones that will help me get to that future state.

One way or another, it's important to find a way to connect to your *why*. It will help give you clarity when you need it and discipline to find motivation when your motivation is lacking.

YOUR COMPASS

More than once I've heard entrepreneurs say, "I don't know what to do next."

The key thing to remember is that you are not looking for

a roadmap. You're looking for a compass. A map tells you exactly where to go. A compass points you in a direction.

No one has an exact plan for you to build your business. In fact, one of the great things about starting a company is the amount of learning you'll experience in trying new things. Sure, there will be minor setbacks—perhaps even major ones. But the compass still points toward your destination.

If you're stuck not knowing what to do, then just do something. Try a different approach. See if that gets you closer to an answer. It's amazing but often true that answers start to present themselves once you are in motion. The universe "conspires" to provide clarity, people, money, and *answers* to those who are pursuing something.

PROCRASTINATION

If you find yourself procrastinating, it helps to get to the root of your motivation. Find your *why*, the reason you started the business. If you started it around an invention or product idea, then tap into your passion for the idea.

If you started your business for work freedom, imagine yourself running your business in an amazing city like Paris or Rio. This desire for freedom was your *why* and it still is. Make it visual. Tack a postcard of Rio on your wall by your desk or put one on your desktop. Ask yourself, "What do I need to do now for twenty five minutes that will help me achieve my goal of running my business in Rio?" Then do it. For twenty five minutes.

There is no perfect time.

There is no perfect plan.

"Step by step. I can't think of any other way of accomplishing anything."

— MICHAEL JORDAN

CHANGING DIRECTION

Many times we feel stuck because what we're doing isn't really working. It could be that the pattern we're in isn't producing the gains we want. It could be that we've explored a few options and those aren't working. This happens quite a bit in the world of startups because startups are basically a series of experiments to prove or disprove a series of hypotheses.

It's like trying to come up with the absolute best recipe for chocolate chip cookies. You'll need to experiment and make batches of cookies with all kinds of different combinations of ingredients, methods, cooking temperatures, baking sheets.

When you feel stuck, you sometimes need to change ingredients or direction. Write it down and talk it out. Writing down what you have tried, tweaking your process, can often reveal alternatives you had not considered. Talking it out with a friend or mentor often brings amazing clarity.

I work with a business coach who will often reverse roles with me. She says, "Okay, you're the coach and I'm the client." When I put my coach hat on, I can figure out my "client's" next few steps and the alternatives. I can also determine the timeframe and action plans.

TOO MUCH TO DO

If you find yourself struggling with endlessly long to-do lists, it's easy to feel overwhelmed. The feeling can be paralyzing and lead to inaction—hours, days, or weeks of putting things off. It's amazingly easy to surf the Internet in procrastination mode because you simply feel overwhelmed.

First-time entrepreneurs are used to having larger organizations to support them, bigger teams, people to pass things to. When you don't have that, you can feel like the weight of the world is on your shoulders, like it's all up to you. In some ways, that's true. The buck does stop with you.

But that doesn't mean you personally need to do it all. One of the hardest things to learn as a new entrepreneur is how to outsource. Find a contractor or a virtual administrator (VA). Don't buy into the myth of the "superman founder."

There are people who are better than you are at many of the tasks on your list. I could have set up my own website. It was a WordPress site and the technical aspects were not that difficult, but I wasn't getting it done. By choosing to outsource it, I was able to pay someone a small amount of money—thus enabling me to focus on things that were more in my own wheelhouse of expertise and joy.

One other thing you can do when you're overwhelmed is go

back to the big picture. Most of the items on your to-do list are not critical to build value in your business.

For Craftsy founder John Levisay, it's about knowing when to say no:

> You have professional maturity, you're focused and can say no to opportunities within your strategic scope, right? The multitude of growth factors within this business could overwhelm the business. Being able to say no to things and focus the team on kind of no more than three to five KPIs [author's note: key performance indicators] or critical success factors, quarterly or even [on an] annual basis, is key. And we make a list every quarter, at the beginning of the year and every quarter, of the things we are going to work on and, more importantly, things we're not going to work on.

What are *the most important* things you should be doing to build value? What are the milestones you need to hit? When do you need to hit them?

Rise above your daily tasks and act like a business advisor, board member, or business coach. If you were looking objectively at the company, what would you advise the founder to focus on? In what time frame?

This kind of objective eye on your business can help eliminate much of the noise.

If you have a hard time seeing your business in this way, ask a friend with solid business insight to take a look and help out.

It's one of the best ways to get unstuck, on track, and back to making progress.

FIND A MEETUP OR PEER GROUP

Entrepreneurship can be a very lonely path. If you're starting your company yourself, it can feel isolating to face all the day-to-day issues on your own. You're probably coming from a larger company where you had friends and colleagues at work.

Even if you have cofounders, being the CEO of a startup company still feels lonely. It can feel overwhelming. You might not feel comfortable sharing everything with your cofounders. The big decisions flow up to you.

Peer groups can be great assets to help overcome these feelings. Startup peer groups are groups of five to ten other CEOs who meet to share issues and support each other. Strict confidentiality is required so that members can share sensitive information about issues they are facing. Most groups are moderated in some way so that discussion flows easily and many topics get covered.

Recall Ben Horowitz's blog about the mean on the test being a twenty two. In that same blog post, he described how tough it is for CEOs to communicate their challenges: "In your darkest moments as CEO, discussing fundamental questions about the viability of your company with your employees can have obvious negative consequences. On the other hand, talking to your board and outside advisors can be fruitless."

Finding a peer group can really help relieve some of this stress and can help you see paths forward that you might not have seen or been willing to embrace. It can be so helpful to talk through issues with people who are going through something similar, or who have had experiences you haven't had yet but might have further down the road.

LEARN THEN ACT

If you're finding that you're stuck in one particular area of your business, look into taking a brief online course about that subject.

With online learning at Udemy, Lynda, Khan Academy, and many others, you can access a huge array of subjects fairly inexpensively and generally move at your own pace.

However, don't fall into a trap of studying and putting off action. Procrastinators love learning because they can put off doing. You have to act on your business challenge as soon as you have the knowledge to do so. You can't let lack of knowledge keep you stuck. The adage "A little knowledge is a dangerous thing" is not true when you're trying to build a startup. In fact, a little knowledge is usually just enough to get you unstuck. So don't let completion of the course, or the next course, keep you from taking timely action.

WRITE IT OUT

Writing about issues and problems that come up can be a helpful tool in getting unstuck. The process of writing can force you to see things you might not have seen before. What are the challenges? What's holding you back from pursuing one of them? If all solutions are imperfect, as they often are in a startup, which one feels like it has the most promise? Why have you not pursued that one?

The acting of writing out issues and challenges helps you to act like your own coach. It's a form of Socratic dialogue that illustrates alternatives and the steps to pursuing a solution. It also helps to shed some light on emotional blockages.

As Edwin Land, founder of Polaroid, said, "If you can state a problem, then you can solve it. From then on, it's just hard work."

It could well be that you know what you need to do but simply aren't doing it. That's a common form of being stuck. So if you do write things out, be honest with yourself about why you're not pursuing one or more courses of action.

Writing things out also lets you work backwards. Start with the end in mind and plan backwards to where you are today. What are the critical things you need to do or learn at each step in order to progress to the next one? When do you plan to achieve those? What steps do you need to take *now* to get to the next step? What is in your way?

LOOK FOR AN ACCOUNTABILITY GROUP

An online or local accountability group comprises people who meet regularly to share goals and encourage and cajole each other. Members hold one another accountable.

I had never used this kind of group before I started blogging and writing my book. I've since found an accountability group extremely helpful in defining my weekly goals. One of the benefits is the regularity of it. Checking in every week makes me plan thoughtfully and consistently.

At the end of each week, the group can shine a light on your progress. Checking in forces you to be honest about whether you accomplished what you set out to do. If you didn't, you're encouraged to look at what might be blocking you. The group can help you identify what might be in your way over time.

An accountability group is different from a peer group in that everyone is committing to the same process.

FIND A COACH

Working with a coach can help accomplish some amazing breakthroughs. A coach can help you articulate and clarify where you are, where you want to be, what your plan is for getting there, and what's in your way.

Coaches are not therapists, though, and you should not think of them that way. Business or life coaches work for you in much the same way sports coaches work with golf and tennis players, maximizing native abilities and devising strategies.

I suggest finding a coach who works with your type of business. You're going to want to interview a few different coaches and find one who fits your style and budget. If you're building a technology startup, find a coach who has worked with technology founders and boards of directors. If you're building a blog or lifestyle business, find a coach who works with writers.

Thanks to Skype and Google Hangouts, you can work with coaches from all over the country and globe—so you don't need to limit yourself to your local area. One blogger friend of mine is a life coach and almost all of his sessions are done through Skype with clients around the world.

GET MOVING AND DO SOMETHING

According to blogger and podcaster Michael Hyatt, "We only begin to get clarity when we get in motion." The universe conspires to help you find an answer after you start moving.

The very act of moving creates a new field of vision, new angles to see things you couldn't when you were still. Ultimately, you have to stop thinking and start doing, even if the first step isn't perfect. If it's in the wrong direction, you can swing around in a quick U-turn. Movement begets other movement.

As motivational speaker Zig Ziglar once said, "You don't drown by falling in water. You only drown if you stay there."

TAKING STOCK & NEXT STEPS

"Life is long if you know how to use it."

LUCIUS ANNAEUS SENECA, ROMAN PHILOSOPHER

At this point in your life, you possess what you need to be a successful founder. And what you don't possess, you can learn. You've developed the personal and professional skills that increase your chances of creating a successful company. As you pursue your startup goals, you'll need to tap into all of your skills at different times in founding and running your business.

Your skills might include:

- Project management
- Financial planning and budgeting
- Negotiating

- Marketing
- Sales
- Engineering
- Hiring
- Managing teams
- Motivating and coaching people
- Presenting to a group or an audience
- Customer relationship building
- Supplier management

When I spoke with Vivek Wadhwa, author of the Kauffman Foundation study that showed successful entrepreneurs are much older than commonly believed, he was adamant that older entrepreneurs are more successful precisely because of their professional experience:

> Building a business is very hard. You have to have a diverse set of skills, everything from financial management to people management to marketing and sales. Sales is something that people don't understand. There is an art to selling, [but] it's a science, not even an art. You have to know how to communicate and inspire and motivate. The young kids don't even know the difference between sales and marketing. How can they? They haven't been out there. They haven't had to sell to succeed yet. All of this comes with experience and negotiating. By the time you're middle-aged, you have negotiated with car dealers, for your house, for everything under the sun.

YOUR ESSENTIAL NETWORK

Your network is one of the most important assets you've

created over your decades of life and work experience. As entrepreneur and author Tim Ferriss says, "Your network is your net worth." Virtually all of the entrepreneurs in this book used their networks extensively for hiring, fundraising, advice, and support.

Plan ahead to map your network to the various needs you're going to have. As an example, you might know people who can help you in certain functions, like marketing, sales, finance, or customer service. They can give you some tips on setting up new functions in those areas. They might know friends and colleagues who are looking for new job opportunities or who can pitch in part time.

You might have people in your network whose overall business acumen you trust and who could be members of your board of directors.

Your network is also there to help you through the rough patches. Schedule social time with friends and former colleagues. Run your ideas past people you trust. Use your network to advise you on key issues.

It's likely that someone in your network can help you with key industry contacts to locate customers, distributors, or other important industry players. If you come from a particular industry, think about all the people you know who can help you. Remember that guy you met at a conference? All the suppliers, customers, or partners you've known through the years? They can be part of your network.

If you still have your day job and your startup is a nights-and-weekends project, you can use that to great benefit. Use the fact that you still have a job as fuel to network like crazy. Having a job is great because you interact regularly with other employees, customers, and vendors—even with competitors. Network inside the company as well as outside. Meet people who can be potential employees, customers, contractors, advisors, mentors, and investors.

These connections are all potentially valuable. You know how it goes with networking: you'll meet someone who knows someone who is *looking right now* for a solution like the one your startup offers.

You also need to begin building your network of entrepreneurs. They are invaluable in finding good contractors, employees, lawyers, and more. They will also help energize you. Entrepreneurs are an incredibly energetic, optimistic group of people. They help each other and push each other to achieve.

Find a Meetup or a LinkedIn group or perhaps a business incubator. If you're not an active and aggressive user of LinkedIn, become one. It's the professional networking tool that helps you keep track of your professional connections. There are premium features available that can also help you make new connections.

As you prepare to start your new business, you want to begin thinking about what you'll need from your network one month, three months, and nine months down the road. Plan now and make the contacts you'll need in advance.

Some people think networking is too "sales-oriented" or too much about asking others for help. But it's much more dynamic and much deeper than that. Networking connects people both socially and professionally. Networks are communities. You've developed yours through decades of working and living.

Your network is your magic. So use it. Remember: if you don't ask, you don't get.

You can use the accompanying chart as a handy tool for helping to define and tap into all the human potential of your network. For each area of expertise, list both close and distant contacts who have skills in that area or who can serve in a particular role. You can add areas of knowledge, skills, and particular needs to the list.

Area	Closest Contacts	Distant Contacts
Idea validation		
Technology, website		
Product development		
Legal		
Marketing		
Sales		
Accounting		
HR		
Customers/prospects		
Advisor		
Industry expertise		
Social		

THE ADVANTAGE OF FAMILY

We know that families take time, energy, effort, and financial support. For me, and for most of the executives I interviewed, however, their families were a key part of their motivation and their support system. There's no emotional and moral support as good as the homegrown kind.

Balancing family obligations and startups is challenging, but it absolutely can be done. Some founders spend less time at home during the crazy formative years. They make that trade-off knowing its limitations, and they make adjustments as they learn to organize their time and set priorities.

Some mid-life entrepreneurs consciously build their businesses around their family obligations. They build a company culture that values personal time and discourages intruding on it. In their years of experience, they've seen businesses that pulled people away from their families and forced them to sacrifice their personal lives.

These founders, like many I interviewed, make conscious choices about doing it differently. They see their kids and spouse as support. They integrate family time and personal "brain clearing" time into the daily fabric of the company.

Some might criticize this approach. They think it implies less commitment and lower expectations for one's company. From what I've seen, and from my conversations with startup founders, this just isn't so.

Lew Cirne built his high-growth software company, New Relic, raising tens of millions in venture capital, and taking it public in 2014. The company raised more than $100 million in its IPO and now has a market value of $1.5 billion. He did all that and still went home at 5:00 every day to cook dinner for his wife and child. He also hired like-minded people and encouraged them to do the same.

YOUR "SHERPAS"

As a founder who's been around the block a few times, you know the value of mentors and guides. Starting a company is a journey. It is filled with wild ups and downs that will test your intellectual, physical, and emotional limits. It's like mountain climbing for which you need a Sherpa—an experienced guide, someone who knows the way.

For me, founding a startup was emotionally taxing. I had a difficult time with those moments in which we didn't know what we were doing—not knowing how to structure my day to tackle a million things, dozens of which seemed like they were really high priority. Being the boss was great but also very lonely. There are so many things you can't tell your employees or your spouse.

You will have real challenges. But the great thing about starting a company later in life is your cache of experience to draw upon. Use your network and set up formal and informal mentoring relationships. You have probably had mentors at different points in your career, even if you didn't call it that. They can be even more valuable at this critical stage when there's so much on the line.

You don't have an office, a water cooler, a company picnic, an annual sales conference, or any of the things that added structure to your workday and work schedule. Mentors, advisors, and business friends can add some structure.

The most effective mentoring involves planning and scheduling regular meetings. Think about what you need from a single mentor or mentor group. Ask for it. Plan for it. Set up your meeting schedule and structure to be sure you get it.

Mentors and advisors are your best sounding board as you work through sticky problems. Your family probably doesn't need or want to hear all the issues, especially all the ups and downs. It's hard enough getting through the founder journey with your family without sharing all the sticky problems. Certain kinds of support are better left to your business advisors.

Advisors can give you honest, unvarnished feedback. Mentors who have gone through the process of starting a company are especially valuable to both guide and prop you up. Ask a hard question and get real answers. Good mentors will help keep you grounded.

YOUR MENTOR CHECKLIST
- What are your business goals? How does this mentor help?
- How do you best communicate with the mentor?
- How frequently should you meet?
- How are you going to prepare for the meetings?
- Is it okay to give the mentor tasks?
- Are you compensating/paying the mentor?

- Are you clear about what the advisor can and cannot share publicly?
- How long do you expect to need this advisor?
- Are they informal advisors or part of an advisory board?

If you're a first-time entrepreneur, you'll have lots of questions and make tons of mistakes. Pick up the phone, shoot a text, or, better yet, see a mentor face to face, and get some guidance.

MANAGING YOUR RISK: THE STAIR STEP METHOD

There is a different way to go about being an entrepreneur than simply "taking the plunge." You can be systematic in learning how to be an entrepreneur and scale your risk as you learn.

Hopefully you have seen some examples and ways to build your business on the side while you keep your day job.

Taylor Pearson, in his book *The End of Jobs,* gives a name to the concept of learning incrementally and adding risk incrementally. He calls it the "stair step method."[38]

Using this method, you build your entrepreneurial skills and relationships over time, trying new business ideas, testing concepts, taking measured risks, and *learning as you go.*

Pearson highlights the example of Rob Walling, who runs multiple software businesses and a successful podcast. Walling quit his corporate job to work as a consultant, learning how to sell his services and the basics of running a small business.

Starting with a very small niche is a great way to get going. You can either add products for that niche or start generating ideas for other markets that you've seen from your experience with your first business.

Building multiple products or multiple businesses over time lets you develop your skills and lets you build key relationships with mentors and contractors. As an example, once you find a great freelance designer, you can work with that person again on your next venture, accelerating your time to market, and letting you test new ideas quickly and inexpensively.

CRANK UP YOUR LEARNING

For entrepreneurs, there's no more important skill than continuous learning. As an entrepreneur, you have to learn the skills you need in real time in order to wear the many hats of a founder.

You'll be learning a lot on the job. You're learning how to start and build a business. You're learning if your product is a fit for your market. You're learning the buying patterns of your customers. You're learning about your partners and distributors.

You'll be testing all of your assumptions, then retesting.

You're going to implement processes for your business based on what you need and what you learn. Much of your learning will be as a result of trial and error. You will probably "achieve" more error in starting a business than you have in any other parts of your life. You need to get comfortable with mistakes because you are going to make a heap of them. The important thing is that you learn each time.

Part of the learning is getting comfortable with setbacks and small failures. The best learning usually comes when things aren't quite working and you need to adjust.

IMPOSTER SYNDROME

"Failure is only failure if it happens in the last chapter. Otherwise, it's a plot twist."

– DANNY INY, BUSINESS CONSULTANT AND BLOGGER

You might have some nagging self-doubt about your ability to get everything done and successfully lead your company. It's a feeling that you aren't good enough, that you're really a fraud, and soon everyone will know it.

It's called "imposter syndrome," and even incredibly talented and successful people have had it, including superstars like Tina Fey and writers like Maya Angelou.

Angelou once said, "I have written eleven books, but each time I think, 'Uh oh, they're going to find out now. I've run a game on everybody, and they're going to find me out.'"

One of the most important ways to overcome imposter syndrome is to stop comparing yourself and your progress to others in startup land. You've heard other entrepreneurs bragging about how they're "killing it." That's easy to say, but it's seldom true.

The fact is that all startups are a series of experiments with frequent failures on the way to a breakthrough. Day to day it might feel like we're failing. Recall Ben Horowitz, founder and CEO of Loudcloud and Silicon Valley venture capital firm Andreessen Horowitz, and his blog post about the "struggle" for CEOs. Everyone feels this struggle, especially because you feel like all the other CEOs are doing so well.

Some of the most successful entrepreneurs I spoke with confessed to feelings of self-doubt despite their years of business experience. For David Mandell, founder and CEO of Pivot-Desk, becoming a company founder was something he worked up to gradually:

> So mine was not a typical entrepreneurial journey, necessarily. I spent the first half of my life/career really in corporate America, and mostly the agency world in New York... [I] worked at a few different agencies...and eventually ended up getting hired by a client of mine who at that point was Deloitte Consulting.

> So, on the agency side, I managed a whole bunch of businesses, mostly of the professional services business-to-business side. But almost every time I was at an agency, I was brought in either to work for someone who then left almost immediately or was brought in to fill an empty spot and was just left to my own devices to build a practice group and that kind of thing. And so I learned a lot about managing and developing people and pushing business objectives...but within a larger corporate structure.

I think what pushed me over the edge were a couple of things...
I was contemplating going back to the agency world, but started
talking to the CEO who started this company that I eventually
ended up joining, and just listening to his passion and the stuff
they were trying to do...and the ability, like the fact that I could
have such an incredible impact, was enough to kind of push me
over the edge. And I always thought, *You know, this is what I've
always been doing, [creating new things] but just for other people.*

It's interesting because it's really been an evolution... This is
my fourth startup. The first one I was one of the first employees...[but] they had already started the company so I wasn't a
cofounder. Obviously I was very early in. My second startup I
started with a cofounder and then brought on a CEO who had a
lot more experience in the startup world and raising capital and
that kind of a thing. The third was I was actually brought in to
run a startup that I had been mentoring that came out of Tech
Stars Boulder, so that was my first CEO gig. But again it wasn't
me starting the company. I wasn't a founder. I was coming into
an existing company to run it. And when that one was over, I
was back in Boulder and trying to figure out what to do next.

And I had this idea, that I was kind of conditioned to think I
needed that initial team... I really got pushed by some of my
future investors, people I knew in the community, and they said,
"Just go do this. You can do this." And so this was really the first
time that I started something by myself. I quickly brought on a
cofounder, but it definitely wasn't, like he was employee number
one, if you know what I mean.

So I went through a real evolution on that process and some

people just get thrown into the deep end early and that's awesome. It was just different for me. I never really considered myself an entrepreneurial person until I got up the guts to leave Deloitte Consulting... I actually left Deloitte to go to the startup world. And it was my first time I really realized, "Holy shit, this is what I've always been doing my whole life—just for other people."

Like so many mid-life entrepreneurs, you might have similar doubts to overcome. Rest assured, it's all part of the process. As Mandell came to understand: "The scariest thing for me...I should say, the two scariest things for me...was first realizing and [then] grasping the belief that you can actually do it."

Don't let imposter syndrome trip you up. You know a lot more than you think you do. When in doubt, throw your energy and focus into getting things done.

NEXT STEPS

You've made it this far and you're convinced that you *should* start a business. You want more control, more wealth, more purpose in life, more capacity to share yourself and your gifts with the world.

But you're just not sure. You've heard lots of talk about risk. A voice inside keeps telling you you're not good enough.

There's a story about a psychologist who asks a group of children, "Who knows how to sing?" Almost all the hands go up. He asks, "Who knows how to paint?" More than half the hands go up. He asks, "Who knows how to dance?" All the hands go up.

The same psychologist asks a group of adults the same questions. Hardly any hands go up for any of the questions.

What happened to the adults? Did they forget how to sing, paint, or dance? Somewhere along the way, they've been convinced they can't do these things.

At this stage of your career, you've probably had enough experience to develop and know your skill set. You know you're a good or even excellent marketing manager, accountant, or salesperson, but could you be a *founder*? That inner voice that has said you can't dance or sing or start a business, that voice is wrong.

In the next ninety days, you can be well on your way to creating a new business that will generate income and wealth, and produce the kind of freedom and purpose you desire.

You can do it whether or not you have a day job, whether or not you have access to funding, and even with all the commitments most people have in mid-life. You simply have to commit to act.

Just for starters, you need plans for thirty, sixty, and ninety days out.

DAYS 1 TO 30

- Talk with your spouse and get his or her support.
- Commit to a schedule for working on your business.
- Begin writing down business ideas. Think about the skills you have, problems you encounter, your current business and network. Generate a few good ideas per day.
- Review the legal documents for your current employer, especially the non-compete and non-solicit sections. Make sure you understand the limitations they impose.
- Take stock of your skills and strengths as well as the ones you don't have and will need to add to.
- Review your network for possible cofounders who will complement your skills.
- Think about and articulate your *"why."*
- Review your idea generation and begin honing in on those ideas you're passionate about, can execute, and for which there's a market.

DAYS 31 TO 60

- Decide on one business idea.
- Create a one-page business plan.
- Approach at least one potential cofounder or decide to go it alone for the right reasons.
- Research contractors who can help you develop the product or overseas factories for sourcing from manufacturers.
- Get your personal finances in order. Understand how much you have to invest in your new business.
- If you're marketing a product, determine your "minimum viable product" (MVP). If it's a service, outline the elements of the service and the pricing.

- Do your Google keyword research into your customers' "pain," what they search for, and what alternatives there are in the market.
- Get a Leadpages account and a Google or Facebook advertising account.
- Begin building a network of other entrepreneurs.
- Know and articulate your goals and schedule.

DAYS 61 TO 90

- Complete a preliminary positioning statement.
- Begin testing your value proposition with small-scale paid advertising using Google or Facebook, driving traffic to a landing page. Start collecting e-mail addresses for prospective customers.
- Go through the culture exercise in Chapter 6 to begin articulating culture and values for your first hires.
- Determine a company name.
- Acquire a URL.
- Set up a basic WordPress website using a pre-bought theme.
- Utilize your network.
- Plan the next ninety days, including delivery of MVP.

At this point, you should be well on your way to creating a business. If things seem to be working, great, keep it up. If not, maybe you need a different idea or a different mode of execution. Keep working at it. Keep in touch with your *why*. Keep building your network. It's your way forward through all the uncertain times.

"You are never too old to set a new goal or to dream a new dream."

— C.S. LEWIS

As I said at the beginning of this guide, you have the hard-earned professional and organizational experience to become a mid-life entrepreneur. You've cultivated a cache of skills to assess, execute, and manage all the details of a new company. What you don't yet know you can learn or delegate to someone who can do it better.

Your talents in management and planning, communication and selling, and marketing and negotiating have all gotten better with time and age. They are invaluable advantages as you start your first company in mid-life or mid-career. And family, it turns out, is more motivation than hindrance.

As you've seen, the highest rates of entrepreneurship are among people fifty five and older. The lowest rates are in the under-thirty-five crowd. You have a leg up on younger founders.

You can go it alone or find partners. You can bootstrap it for a time before raising funds. You can keep your day job and start your business on the side. Along any path you choose, you'll be tapping into your network of advisors and mentors, family, colleagues, and friends to get the support and expertise you need to succeed.

So what are you waiting for?

"If not now, when?"

— RABBI HILLEL

It is my sincere hope that, in your reading of this guide, you've come to know that you, too, can live your entrepreneurial dream. I hope you've discovered that it's *Never Too Late to Startup.*

ACKNOWLEDGMENTS

———

I owe the deepest of thanks to my family for their love and support, especially my wife Suzie.

Thanks also to those who kept me on track, including my coach Vikki Munroe and my BLF Accountability Mastermind team. Special thanks to my friend Sam, whose seemingly innocent comment, "I need your book," served as a motivational rallying cry.

So much of this book was dependent on extensive interviews with founders and other supporters of entrepreneurship. I am so grateful for the time and expertise these talented people so generously shared. The interviews were conducted in 2014 and 2015. Thanks to:

Van Barker
Josh Becker
Joe BelBruno

Lew Cirne
Kelly Cooper
Walter Cruttenden
Tim Enwall
Brad Feld
John Gilluly
Scott Granai
Eric Groves
Brad Handler
John Levisay
Dan Malven
David Mandell
Jack O'Toole
Art Papas
Sean Reilly
Sara Schaer
Jo Tango
Vivek Wadhwa

NOTES

1. Woolhouse, Megan, citing Robert Pollin, *The Boston Globe*, October 29, 2015, https:// www.bostonglobe.com/business/2015/10/29/where-jobs-are-and-aren/ yEpsJFw31MzfCLJ4hpcTYO/story.html

2. Hamilton Project, http://www.hamiltonproject.org/multimedia/charts/ the_rising_cost_of_college

3. Rayfield, Nicholas, *USA Today*, April 8, 2015, http://college.usatoday. com/2015/04/08/ national-student-loan-debt-reaches-a-bonkers-1-2-trillion/

4. Leonhardt, David, *The New York Times*, May 27, 2014, http://www.nytimes. com/2014/05/27/upshot/is-college-worth-it-clearly-new-data-say.html

5. Meeker, Mary, *Internet Trends Report*, 2015, http://www.kpcb.com/ internet-trends

6. Stangler, Dane, "The Coming Entrepreneurship Boom," 2009, http://www.kauffman.org/what-we-do/research/2009/07/ the-coming-entrepreneurship-boom

7. Pink, Daniel, *Drive: The Surprising Truth About What Motivates Us*, Riverhead Books, 2009

8. Graham, Paul, http://www.paulgraham.com/die.html

9. Wasserman, Noam, *The Founder's Dilemmas*, Princeton University Press, 2012

10. Horowitz, Ben, *Ben's Blog*, http://www.bhorowitz.com/
    what_s_the_most_difficult_ceo_skill_managing_your_own_psychology

11. MarketingCharts.com, April 9, 2015, http://www.marketingcharts.com/online/
    retail-e-commerce-roundup-market-shares-attractiveness-and-more-53439/

12. Raymundo, Oscar, *Inc. Magazine*, http://www.inc.com/oscar-raymundo/eric-
    bandholz-beardbrand-beard-grooming-products.html

13. Internet Advertising Bureau, IAB.net, http://www.iab.net/about_the_iab/
    recent_press_releases/press_release_archive/press_release/pr-061115

14. Wikipedia.org, https://en.wikipedia.org/wiki/Bryan_Johnson_entrepreneur

15. Wasserman, Noam, *The Founder's Dilemmas*, Princeton University Press, 2012

16. Wikipedia.org, https://en.wikipedia.org/wiki/Spanx

17. Ibid.

18. Wikipedia.org, https://en.wikipedia.org/wiki/Richard_Branson

19. Altucher, James, *Choose Yourself*, Lioncrest Publishing, 2013

20. McClure, Dave, http://www.slideshare.net/
    dmc500hats/ everything-sucks-and-nobody-cares

21. Linkner, Josh, *Fast Company*, March 27, 2012, http://www. fastcompany.
    com/1826271/your-company-selling-aspirin-or-vitamins

22. Blank, Steve, *Four Steps to the Epiphany*, K&S Ranch, 2003

23. Graham, Paul, *Do Things That Don't Scale*, http://paulgraham.com/ds.html

24. Hoffman, Reid, *VentureBeat.com*, lecture at Stanford University,
    November 4, 2014, http://venturebeat.com/2014/11/06/
    how-linkedins-reid-hoffman-taught-stanford-students-to-build-billion-dollar-
    businesses-through-personal-networks-in-4-quotes/

25. Zuckerberg, Mark, Excerpt from Facebook Town Hall Q&A
    with Mark Zuckerberg, http://newsroom.fb.com/news/2014/11/
    highlights-from-qa-with-mark

26. Wasserman, Noam, *The Founder's Dilemmas*, Princeton University Press, 2012

27. Suster, Mark, *Both Sides of the Table*, May 9, 2011, http://www.bothsidesofthetable.com/2011/05/09/the-co-founder-mythology/

28. Kawasaki, Guy, blog post on LinkedIn pulse, November 24, 2014, *The Art of Finding a Cofounder*

29. Lean Canvas licensed under Creative Commons Attribution-Share Alike 3.0 Un-ported License

30. Carlson, Nicholas, "Inside Groupon", *Business Insider*, http://www.businessinsider.com/inside-groupon-the-truth-about-the-worlds-most-controversial-company-2011-10

31. Godin, Seth, http://sethgodin.typepad.com/seths_blog/2008/01/permission-mark.html

32. Kauffman Foundation, *How Entrepreneurs Access Capital and Get Funded*, 2015, http://www.kauffman.org/ what-we-do/resources/entrepreneurship-policy-digest/ how-entrepreneurs-access-capital-and-get-funded

33. Suster, Mark, *Both Sides of the Table*, September 20, 2009, http://www.bothsidesofthetable.com/2009/09/20/i-met-with-an-investor-what-happens-next/

34. Bruder, Jessica, *Inc. Magazine*, June 2014, http://www.inc.com/magazine201406/jessica-bruder/how-to-balance-company-and-marriage.html

35. Danigelis, Alyssa, *Inc. Magazine*, interview with Brad Feld, October 8, 2010, http://www.inc.com/articles/2010/10/brad-feld-goes-off-the-grid.html

36. *Pediatrics*, March 10, 2014, Jenny S. Radesky, MD, Caroline J. Kistin, MD, MsC, Barry Zuckerman, MD, Katie Nitzberg, BS, Jamie Gross, Margot Kaplan-Sanoff, EdD, Marilyn Augustyn, MD, and Michael Silverstein, MD MP

37. Foster, Tom, "The Startup That Conquered Facebook Sales," *Inc. Magazine*, June 2014

38. Pearson, Taylor, *The End of Jobs*, Lioncrest Publishing, 2015

ABOUT THE AUTHOR

—

ROB KORNBLUM has spent twenty-five years funding, supporting, advising, and founding new companies, helping to grow businesses in a diverse range of industries including technology, health care, consumer services, and media.

He is a former venture capitalist and Kauffman Fellow, a growth company executive, and startup founder. He has appeared in *The Huffington Post*, *Inc.* magazine, Business.com, and numerous blogs. Rob lives in the Boston area with his wife and three sons.